WORLD CRICKET GROUNDS

WORLD CRICKET GROUNDS

A PANORAMIC VISION

Michael Heatley

COMPENDIUM

First published in 2009 by Compendium Publishing Ltd.

COMPENDIUM

ISBN: 978-1-905573-01-1

Design: Danny Gillespie - Compendium Publishing

Printed and bound in China

PAGE 1: West Indies' Marlon Samuels fields near the boundary as storm clouds pass overhead during the World Cup match against New Zealand at St Johns on Antigua. *Tim Wimborne/Reuters/Corbis 42-18134685*

PAGES 2–3: Lumley Castle overlooks the Riverside during day three of the Fourth Test between England and the West Indies on 17 June 2007. The home side is on its way to 400. *Mike Hewitt/Getty Images 74690817*

RIGHT: Lord's Cricket Ground on July 12, 2008. *Tom Shaw/Getty Images 81914307*

CONTENTS

HAROLD 'DICKIE' BIRD MBE

Born: 19 April 1933
Career: Yorkshire 1956–1959; Leicestershire 1959–1964
First-class debut: 16 May 1956 (Yorkshire v Scotland
Last first-class match: 12 August 1964 (Leicestershire v Essex)
Umpiring career: County debut 1970; Test debut 1973 (66 tests and 69 ODIs umpired)
Batting career: 93 first-class matches, 170 innings, 3,314 runs, average 20.71 (2 hundreds, 14 fifties), top score 181*

Memorable moments:
1933 Born in Barnsley
1956 First match for Yorkshire
1959 Makes top career score of 181* against Glamorgan
1959 First match for Leicestershire
1970 Umpires in first county game
1973 Umpires in first test match (against New Zealand at Leeds)
1996 Officiates in last test, England v India
1997 *My Autobiography* published: becomes a best-seller with over 500,000 copies sold
1998 Officiates in last county match

The world of cricket has changed radically in the last few years: a new form of the game—Twenty20 cricket—has taken the world by storm and in the Indian Premier League has seen players valued at sums of money that would have seemed a fantasy to cricketers of older generations.

There have been other changes that, while not as obvious, have affected the way that cricket is played, and many of these have involved the umpires. Not always the favourite people on the pitch, umpires are an essential element of cricket and—in common with referees or any form of sporting 'policemen'—it is essential that their authority is complete. It was for this reason in 2002 that the ICC ruled that both umpires in test matches must be neutral. Before then there had always been the suspicion that it was not just the laws of cricket that led to the umpire's finger being raised, but something known to players of all forms of cricket from grassroots up—home team umpiring.

Television replays did not help as they exposed umpiring mistakes to a glare of scrutiny. Run outs, LBW decisions, catches: all of these have been routinely picked over by television pundits, frame by frame, since computer analysis has become more sophisticated. As in so many other sports, the use of these replays soon became part of the game. Run outs became the province of an official in the stands. In many cases these were straightforward, but even television could not always be sure.

Today, predictive technology allows computer assessments of a ball's line and height and is regularly used on television to dissect LBW decisions. This unforgiving practice has led to another change for umpires. Used in earlier Sri Lanka v India and the New Zealand v West Indies series, in the recent England tour of the West Indies, players were allowed to challenge umpiring results which were then decided by television replay and the use of Hawkeye technology.

Has this technology improved matters for umpires or not? It's a difficult question to answer: overturning decisions as a result of a television replay is bound to have an effect—although it may have come as a surprise to some batsmen that the umpires got it right more often than they expected!

Possibly the most hated technology used by umpires came with the advent of light meters. Even the most popular of umpires have felt the force of spectator anger when play has been suspended for bad light, although it was a waterlogged pitch that caused problems in 1980 when David Constant and 'Dickie' Bird kept the players of the pitch during the centenary test at Lord's.

In spite of these hardships and changing times, there are umpires who have always been held in high esteem—umpires such as 'Dickie' Bird, whose test career spanned nearly 25 years, and for whom umpiring provided an involvement in cricket at the highest level that his professional cricketing career could not.

'Dickie' Bird officiated in a then-record 66 tests and 69 ODIs and visited many of the cricket grounds shown in this book. As an umpire he was never keen to give an LBW decision unless he was certain it was out: and all cricketers will attest to the vagaries of the path of a cricket ball for all clearcut lines of modern technology.

RIGHT: 'Dickie' Bird seen officiating at the Texaco Trophy match against the West Indies at the Oval, 26 May 1995.
Popperfoto/Getty Images 78964114

INTRODUCTION

A report in *Wisden* of the annual Eton v Harrow cricket match in 1872 revealed that 'Never before was congregated on Lord's Ground so numerous and brilliant a company...' and 'The crush at the gates on the first day was great and lasting beyond all precedent...' An unthinkable happening today for a meeting of the two public schools but symptomatic of how popular organised cricket was when still in its relative infancy—and how passionate a following it could create. History tells us that often, the venue itself, as with football grounds, has been responsible for creating a mystical atmosphere which can both intimidate and inspire.

The close proximity of a crowd, its sheer volume or imposing topography are just a sample of those elements which give certain venues their unique qualities. Lord's, the largest of English grounds, can be a daunting proposition for the rookie cricketer simply due to its history, while the Melbourne Cricket Ground and the Eden Gardens in Kolkata (Calcutta) trade on sheer size. By contrast, the smaller, more intimate grounds often prove to be a more pleasurable experience for spectator and player alike.

But whatever a ground has to offer by way of atmosphere or history financial considerations are increasingly taking over. In the twenty-first century, the sport's followers are being asked to part with substantial sums of cash to support their chosen teams and, whether in Australia, South Africa or England, fans are seeking facilities which warrant those spiralling prices. The quality of the cricket is not the only criterion—the venues have to match.

Expenditure becomes a major issue as soon as an announcement is made for the location of a forthcoming World Cup; the costs and games have often been spread over more than one country. Also, it can lead to questions being posed as to whether certain grounds are up to the task at hand; the famous Bourda in Guyana was rejected as a World Cup venue in 2007 because of the lack of modern facilities. Modern purpose-built venues or lack of investment may sound the death knell of many traditional arenas.

Another problem remains the underuse of grounds, although the more commercially aware operations will offer hospitality facilities, share with other sports (as is typical in the southern hemisphere) or stage concerts which often attract more people than the cricket.

It can sometimes transpire that the conditions for playing and viewing the game appear far superior in less celebrated venues than the more established grounds. Lack of spectators in what we might regard as hotbeds of cricket can also be an eye-opener. And, although test series like the titanic 2005 Ashes struggle prove there is a large audience for the game in its purest form, it's undoubtedly the case that the one-day and Twenty20 versions often bring in much larger crowds than the full-length game. This latter problem has of course nothing to do with amenities and is all about the spectators' appetite for excitement allied to definite results. But even (or maybe especially) those who prefer 'instant' cricket demand modern facilities.

Another issue to have come into play in recent years is security, a major problem in India, Pakistan and Sri Lanka. For those countries terrorism is a very real threat and armed police or army personnel can be found both in and outside the grounds. Certain venues have not proved to be as attractive a proposition to touring sides as in the past. The possibility of terrorist attacks is not, of course, confined to that part of the world and increased vigilance was evident during the Australian tour of England in 2005. The events in Mumbai in 2008 exacerbated this even more.

The question of crowd control could be viewed as another side of the same coin, for there is no question that there are elements of 'football-fan' behaviour creeping into cricket. The popularity of the one-day game at all levels has been partly to blame and has attracted the type of person who will often reject the values of the three and five-day game.

The revamping of the area in front of the Lord's Tavern due to unruly behaviour may only be an isolated case, but action has been taken at other grounds around the world to nullify those would seek to make watching cricket a less than pleasurable experience. Thankfully, cricket crowds remain generally less boisterous than their footballing counterparts, even when drink is taken, and segregation of fans is rarely considered.

Cricket authorities the world over are constantly in search of extra revenue and the money that satellite TV giant Sky has ploughed into the game for test match rights in recent years has been gratefully received, although many have argued against the deal. The important factor remains how this revenue is spent but somewhere along the line ground improvement has to be taken into consideration. With fans around the globe now able to view cricket at the highest level almost on a weekly basis, their familiarity with overseas venues becomes more acute and new innovations/facilities are there to be seen. If a ground in South Africa or Australia takes on a new facade there is every chance that the modern cricket fan in another part of the world will expect the same.

Thanks to Peter Gamble for the research; and to *Wisden* and, in particular, the brilliant online www.cricinfo.com for the stats.

RIGHT: The travelling English supporters, the Barmy Army, at the Gabba November 27, 2006. *Philip Brown/Corbis 42-17609507*

LEFT: Indian cricket team members wave to the crowd during a bustop victory procession in Mumbai. Thousands of fans filled the road to welcome the team on their way back from South Africa after winning the Twenty20 World Cup by beating Pakistan in the final. *STR/epa/Corbis 42-18973337*

RIGHT: Spectators sit in front of the scoreboard at Kingston, Jamaica during the drawn test between the West Indies and Australia, 1991. The great West Indian team of the 1980s would break up in the 1990s, but was still strong enough to beat the Australians 2–1 with Richie Richardson the pick of the batsmen (475 runs at 67.85) and Malcolm Marshall the best bowler (21 wickets at 20.80). Note the name of the twelfth man—Brian Lara, then 21 and in the process of breaking into the team. Two years later on the West Indian winning (2–1) tour of Australia, Lara, in his fifth test, would score his maiden test century—a small matter of 277. *David Cumming; Eye Ubiquitous/Corbis UB001437*

AUSTRALIA

This fabulous panoramic view of the Melbourne Cricket Ground is made from four images merged together. They were taken on 15 December 2002 during the VB Trination Series ODI between Australia and England. Note building work at right: the redevelopment of the stadium was finished for the 2006 opening of the Commonwealth Games. *Tom Shaw/Getty Images 1747042*

ADELAIDE OVAL

ADELAIDE OVAL

Address: North Adelaide, Adelaide, South Australia
Website: www.cricketsa.com.au
Capacity: c32,000
Opening Date: 1873

Memorable moments:

1884 First test at the Oval, Australia v England, played 12–16 December. England won by eight wickets after R. Peel takes 5–51 in Australia's second innings

1895 A.E. Trott takes 8–43 allowing Australia to beat England, for the first time at Adelaide, by 382 runs

1932 D.G. Bradman scores 299* against South Africa

1932–33 The third test of the infamous 'Bodyline' tour sees W.A.S. Oldfield and W.M. Woodfull injured but Australia level the series at 1–1, winning by 111 runs thanks to Bill O'Reilly's match analysis of 10–129

1948 Australia score 674 (D.G. Bradman 201, A.L. Hassett 198), still highest test innings score on the ground

1951 Australia all out for 82 against West Indies, the lowest test total by any side on ground. F.M.M. Worrell took 6–38

1975 First ODI at the Oval, Australia v West Indies, on 20 December. Australia win by five wickets

2003 R.T. Ponting scores 242 against India, one of five hundreds he's scored at Adelaide (the most by any player)

2006 P.D. Collingwood (206) and K.P. Pietersen (158) put on 4th-wicket record of 310 out of England's 551–6d—but Australia win the match

When reading any description of the Adelaide Oval, the word 'picturesque' will inevitably be used somewhere along the line. Situated amongst trees and gardens, with St Peter's Cathedral alongside to complete the canvas, that's exactly what it is. Redevelopment—most recently the addition of the Chappell stands—has been carefully tailored.

Home to the South Australian state side, the ground has hosted many sports in its history, although in very early days the quality of the cricket pitches was always a matter for concern. This was due to having to share facilities with an Australian Rules team at a time when the science of pitch preservation was not even in its infancy.

On the playing front the Oval has witnessed its fair share of controversy, most notably when the famed 'Bodyline' issue came to a head at the ground in 1933.

In terms of structure there are many pleasing features, including the Sir Donald Bradman Stand, completed in 1980; this was designed to complement the existing George Giffin, Sir Edwin Smith and Mostyn Evan stands on the western side of the ground which are listed as historic sites by Adelaide Heritage. Opposite these can be found the Chappell Stands, built in 2003. It should also be noted that the pitch constitutes a true oval.

Bradman, who represented both New South Wales and South Australia, played his final match at Adelaide in March 1949 and various pieces of memorabilia associated with 'The Don' and other cricketing greats can be found in the cricket museum under the stand that bears his name.

RIGHT: The Adelaide Oval during the ING Cup match between the Southern Redbacks and the Western Warriors 17 December 2004. Architect Kenneth Milne designed the scoreboard which first saw service on 3 November 1911. The clock was added in 1912 and the windvane in the 1930s. At right a tower of St Peter's, the Anglican cathedral that gives its name to the 'Cathedral End'. *Sean Garnsworthy/Getty Images 51874031*

ABOVE: Game six of the Commonwealth Bank ODI series between New Zealand and England on 23 January 2007 was a day/night fixture that New Zealand won by 90 runs. *Clive Rose/Getty Images 73080785*

RIGHT: Day three of the Fourth Test between Australia and India on 26 January 2008. At left—the Eastern side of the ground—the new Chappell Stands which were constructed in 2003. *Robert Cianflone/Getty Images 79265711*

LEFT: This view of Adelaide Oval on 27 November 2001 shows well the changes the last decade have brought. At left, the seating that would give way to the Chappell Stands; at right, the Bradman Stand. The game is the Pura Cup match between the Southern Redbacks and the Western Warriors. *Tony Lewis/Allsport/Getty Images 999625*

BRISBANE CRICKET GROUND

BRISBANE CRICKET GROUND (THE GABBA)

Address: Woolloongabba, Brisbane, Queensland
Website: www.thegabba.com.au
Capacity: c42,000
Opening Date: 1895

Memorable moments:

1931 The Gabba's first test, Australia v South Africa, during which D.G. Bradman scored 226, still the top test score on the ground

1946 Australia score 645 (D.G. Bradman 187, A.L. Hassett 128) v England, the highest test total on the ground

1947 India skittled for 58 (E.R.H. Toshack 2.3-1-2-5)

1960 First Test between Australia (505 and 232) and West Indies (453 and 284) ended in a tie after the last-gasp runout of I. Meckiff, one of three such dismissals. Wes Hall took 5–63

1979 First ODI, England v West Indies, played on 23 December; West Indies win by nine wickets

1985 R.J. Hadlee takes 9–52 and 6–71 and New Zealand score 553 (M.D. Crowe 188, J.F. Reid 108) to win by an innings and 41 in spite of a stand of 197 for the sixth wicket by A.R. Border (152*) and G.R.J. Matthews (115)

1992 Australia win World Cup match against India by one run when Raju was run out on the last ball

2004 Australia's innings of 585 against New Zealand includes two ground record partnerships—216 (M.J. Clarke 141, A.C. Gilchrist 126) for the sixth and 114 (G.D. McGrath 61, J.N. Gillespie 54*) for the tenth wicket

2006 First T20I, Australia v South Africa, played on the ground—and in Australia—on 9 January

Although 1895 is the recognised date for the establishment of the Brisbane Cricket Ground, it was not until the following year that it witnessed its first fixture when a Parliamentary team took on the Press. It then took until 1931 before test and Sheffield Shield fixtures became a regular feature.

The Gabba (so called because of its Woolloongabba location) is home to both the Queensland cricket team and the Brisbane Lions Aussie Rules side and, after years of neglect, has seen some dramatic changes during the last decade or so. First was the disappearance of the greyhound-racing track in 1993, which allowed the pitch dimensions to exceed those of the Melbourne Cricket Ground.

The erection of a number of new stands then took place, the Northern Stand opening in 1995 to be followed four years later by its Eastern, Western and Southern counterparts. The reconstruction project came to its conclusion in 2005 when Queensland Prime Minister Peter Beattie opened the grandstand which had replaced the old Lions Social Club.

During the upheaval, the playing area had also acquired new turf in keeping with the requirements of a 21st Century cricket venue. Local cricket followers would no doubt suggest that the $100 million plus is money well spent.

In addition to the aforementioned sports, The Gabba has been used for baseball, cycling, rugby union and athletics. The official attendance record is 47,096 for a rugby league test in 1954 between Australia and Great Britain.

RIGHT: Steve Harmison bowls a wide for the first ball of the First Test on 23 November 2006. The left-hand field is set for Justin Langer who went on to score 82 in the first innings and 100* in the second as Australia won by 277 runs. *Philip Brown/Corbis 42-17599830*

LEFT: Two days later, a packed house enjoys the action during day three of the same match. *Cameron Spencer/Getty Images 72641473*

LEFT: 23 November 2000 and Glenn McGrath is applauded from the field by his team mates after taking 6–17 and helping skittle out the West Indies for 82 during the first day's play of the First Test. By close of play Australia were 107–1 and on their way to an innings' victory. *Nick Wilson/Allsport/Getty Images 1086874*

RIGHT: The First Test of Pakistan's 1999–2000 tour of Australia saw a 10-wicket loss. This view of the Gabba was taken on the last day of the match, 9 November 1999, during Australia's canter to victory. G.S. Blewett (40*) and M.J. Slater (32*) knocking off the 74 needed for victory. Note the 24-bay gap where the Brisbane Lions Australian Football Social Club once stood. The redevelopment was completed in 2005. *Jack Atley/Getty Images 3017662*

MELBOURNE CRICKET GROUND

MELBOURNE CRICKET GROUND

Address: Jolimont, Melbourne, Victoria
Website: www. mcg.org.au
Capacity: 100,000
Opening Date: 1854

Memorable moments:
1877 First ever test match played between Australia and England 15–19 March. Australia (245 and 104) beat England (196 and 108) by 45 runs
1912 J.B. Hobbs and W. Rhodes put on 323 for first wicket, still the record ground partnership
1932 South Africa dismissed for 36 and 45 (Ironmonger match analysis of 22.5-12-24-11) the two lowest scores at the MCG
1937 D.G. Bradman (270) and J.H.W. Fingleton (136) and put on 346 for the sixth, a ground test record for any wicket
1937 Australia score 604 (D.G. Bradman 169, S.J. McCabe 112, C.L. Badcock 118) against England, the highest test match total on the ground
1951 Australia's fourth-innings last-wicket partnership of 38 by D.T. Ring (30*) and W.A. Johnston (7*) beats the West Indies by one wicket
1961 A single-day attendance of 90,800 was recorded during the Test versus the West Indies
1966 Bob Cowper scores 307 (out of 543–8d) against England, the highest test score at the MCG
1971 First ODI, Australia v England, played 5 January
2001 A.C. Gilchrist (98) and M.E. Waugh (112*) put on 206 for the first wicket in an ODI against the West Indies and Australia win by nine wickets at a canter
2008 First T20I, Australia v India, played 1 February

The Melbourne Cricket Ground (MCG) is unquestionably the major sporting venue in Australia, having been the location for countless cricket tests and Australian Rules finals. The 1956 Olympic Games were centred at the ground and the final touches were added for the 2006 Commonwealth Games, hosted by Melbourne. Anyone who saw the fabulous opening celebrations will think that the $450 million facelift was worthwhile. However, the success of this development has led people—particularly the Australian Football League—to push for a similar upgrading of the Great Southern Stand.

To those outside Australia, the MCG is synonymous with cricket, its vast stands and intimidating atmosphere felt by visiting teams. The reduction in capacity from 125,000 to the present figure of 100,000 is no help to the debutant batsman. There may have been many criticisms about the quality of the pitches in the latter part of the last century, but the MCG remains a magnificent arena.

During its history the MCG has seen many alterations in its structure, the building of the mammoth Great Southern Stand, completed in 1992 and seating over 44,000 spectators being one of the most dramatic changes in recent years. Inevitably, chunks of history disappear with redevelopment, leading to the demise of the 1956-built Olympic Stand, the Pavilion and the much loved Ponsford Stand, all falling victim to the bulldozer in the run-up to the Commonwealth Games.

RIGHT: The MCG stands are empty during the Ford Ranger Cup match between the Victorian Bushrangers and the Queensland Bulls on 6 February 2007. *Lucas Dawson/Getty Images 79576338*

LEFT: When packed, as seen here during the fourth Ashes test match on 26 December 2006, the MCG can hold nearly 100,000—the sort of audience that few cricket matches enjoy. In February 1961, 90,800 turned up to watch the West Indies play Australia; on 26 December 2006, ABC News reported the figure of 89,155 was the 'biggest ever for a single day of a test between England and Australia and also the highest Boxing Day attendance'. The test was also the 100th at the MCG and saw Shane Warne take his 700th wicket when he bowled Strauss for 50—the milestone that helped prompt the high audience figure. *Philip Brown/Corbis 42-17740030*

FOLLOWING PAGES:
What a difference! Seen in 1955 (**LEFT**) before the Olympic Games of 1956, Melbourne looks very different. This view (**RIGHT**) shows the massive changes that have brought the ground up to modern standards, capable of holding huge crowds over a range of sports. Australian Football holds the record attendance—121,696 at the 1970 Carlton v Collingwood grand final. At left, over the railway lines, are the Vodafone and Rod Laver arenas. *Doug Byrnes/Corbis U1278669INP; Getty Images 42-19792814*

LEFT: The MCG has seen plenty of redevelopment over the years to maintain and improve audience facilities. In this 2004 view, the VB Series ODI between Australia and India takes place before the partially demolished Members Stand. *Hamish Blair/Getty Images 2854298*

RIGHT: A 1992 view of the MCG during the final of the Cricket World Cup between England and Pakistan that Pakistan won by 22 runs. *Adrian Murrell/Getty Images1246985*

PERTH—WESTERN AUSTRALIA CRICKET ASSOCIATION GROUND

WACA GROUND

Address: East Perth, Perth, Western Australia,
Website: www.waca.com.au
Capacity: 20–24,000
Opening Date: 1890

Memorable moments:

1970 First test played at the WACA—Australia v
England 11–16 December. It ends as a draw after
centuries by B.W. Luckhurst (131), I.R. Redpath
(171), G.S. Chappell (108), and J.H. Edrich (115*)

1980 First ODI, India v New Zealand, played on
9 December

1981 Pakistan all out 62 (D.K. Lillee 5–18) for ground's
lowest test innings total

1988 M.G. Hughes takes a ground's best match analysis
of 13–217 but this doesn't stop the West Indies
winning by 169 runs

1999 R.T. Ponting (197) and J.L. Langer (144) put on
327—a ground test record—for the fifth wicket
against Pakistan

2003 Australia's M.L. Hayden makes a massive 380
(out of 735–6d) against Zimbabwe, which consti-
tuted a test record at the time, and continues to
be the highest score at the ground

2004 G.D. McGrath takes 8–24 against Pakistan as
they slump to 72 all out chasing 564

2005 Australia's first ever Twenty20 match between
the Western Warriors and the Victorian
Bushrangers saw over 20,000 spectators
crammed into the ground

2007 First T20I, Australia v New Zealand, played 11
December

Swampland may not the obvious location to attempt to establish a cricket ground but the Western Australia Cricket Association (WACA) established the WACA ground in 1890 in a brave reclamation project. It would be take another three years before the official opening and a further year before cricket truly established itself.

Due to its relative isolation on the west coast, the WACA only became a Test venue after regular scheduled flights were introduced, England the initial visitors in 1970. The home to the Western Australia state side was shared by Australian Rules from 1987 to 2000 before football emigrated to a larger stadium close by, and rugby league made a brief appearance during the 1990s.

Efforts have been made in recent times to improve facilities at a venue which has struggled to pay its way. In 2002, the erection of a new grandstand and players' pavilion went some way to solving the problems, while seats were removed on both sides of the ground to be replaced by sloping grassed areas and the playing area reduced in size. This improved facilities but reduced the overall capacity of the ground—although temporary stands are erected to bring capacity up to 24,000 as necessary.

Cricket matches at the WACA have never been short of incident. Apart from Hayden's record innings, Dennis Lillee introduced his infamous aluminium bat in 1979—an incident that would be hard to beat in headline-grabbing terms. And let's not forget Glenn McGrath's 300th test wicket against the West Indies in 2000, when he completed a hat-trick in the process.

RIGHT: 22,000 fans watch the action during day four of the third Ashes test between Australia and England on 17 December 2006. After Australia's fine second innings total of 527–5d (M.J. Clarke 135*, M.E.K. Hussey 103, A.C. Gilchrist 102*, M.L. Hayden 92) England were set 557 to win. They struggled from 19–1 to 265–5 in 96 overs to day 4, but tumbled to 350 all out the next day. *Ezra Shaw/Getty Images 72838552*

LEFT: High-angle view of play during day one of the Third Test between Australia and India at the WACA on 16 January 2008. India ended the day on 296–6. The two grassy hills created by the last ground development are clearly visible on either side of the pitch at midwicket and cover. *Paul Kane/Getty Images 79012124*

ABOVE: The WACA's six light towers stand 70 metres above the ground and were first used in 1986. Under the light at left is the Inverarity Stand, named for John Inverarity who captained Western Australia to the Sheffield Shield title four times in five years. To the right is the Prindiville Stand, named after former WACA President Bernie. *Robert Garvey/Corbis VY001331*

SYDNEY CRICKET GROUND

SYDNEY CRICKET GROUND

Address: Paddington, Sydney, New South Wales
Website: www.sydneycricketground.com.au
Capacity: 40,000
Opening Date: 1876

Memorable moments:

1882 First test, Australia v England, played 17–21 February—the sixth ever test match, Australia wins by 5 wickets

1888 Australia's 42 (G. Lohmann 5–17, R. Peel 5–18) is still the ground's lowest test innings total

1903 R.E. Foster scores the ground's highest test innings of 287 and England win by five wickets

1930 Donald Bradman scores 452* for New South Wales against Queensland, then the world record for first-class cricket. He made his runs in only 415 minutes!

1946 S.G. Barnes and D.G. Bradman scored 234 apiece as Australia amassed a score of 659 against England in, 405 for the fifth wicket

1979 The ground's first ODI played between Australia and England, 13 January

2004 India 705–7d is the ground's highest total and S.R. Tendulkar (241) and V.V.S. Laxman (178) put on a record partnership of 353 for the fourth wicket

2007 First T20I, Australia v England, on 9 January

2008 A. Symonds (162*) and G.B. Hogg (79) put on a ground test record 173 for the seventh wicket in a high scoring match against India that sees four other centuries (V.V.S. Laxman 109, S.R. Tendulkar 154, M.L. Hayden 123, M.E.K. Hussey 145*). Australia win by 122 runs

The official opening date for the Sydney Cricket Ground is open to debate, but the first SCG was established in 1876: the NSW–Victoria match three years later signalled the arrival of first-class cricket, test matches arriving in 1882. However records show that a cricket pitch was in place as early as 1810, a match being played in 1854 at a time when the environs were home to the British Army.

Serious construction work took place throughout the 1880s and 1890s, the Members' Pavilion taking on a new look in 1886 and the Ladies' Stand coming to fruition in 1896. By 1903 the Northern Stand, the Members' Stand extension, the lighting and new scoreboard were in place.

In the first quarter of the 20th century the SCG witnessed both association football and rugby league, while the 1938 Empire Games were staged there.

The Northern Stand had long gone when the Bradman Stand was completed in 1973, the addition of new floodlights in 1978 and the new Brewongle Stand of 1980 continuing the commitment to change. An electronic scoreboard, what is now the O'Reilly stand and the Clive Churchill Stand all changed the nature of the SCG during the 1980s. Further redevelopment—planned to be ready for the 2010–11 Ashes tour—will see improvements to the Noble and Bradman stands and removal of the Dally Messenger Stand.

Rugby league and soccer found a new home during the upheaval but were replaced by AFL team the Sydney Swans, who now co-exist amicably with the cricketing New South Wales Blues.

RIGHT: Spectators watch play during the Commonwealth Bank ODI Series second final match between Australia and England on 11 February 2007. The football ground (opened in 1988; today holds 45,000) is at right. The two green-roofed buildings are the Ladies' Stand (L) and the Members' Pavilion. The stand to left of the Ladies is the Brewongle Stand, named, it is said, after an Aboriginal camping ground. To the right of the pavilion is M.A. Noble stand, whose derivation is better known: Monty Noble (1873–1940) was a great New South Wales and Australian captain. *Ezra Shaw/Getty Images 73288127*

PREVIOUS PAGES: This 1990s picture shows Sydney's Moore Park stadium complex. Aussie Stadium‹the Sydney Football Stadium‹is at left and the Sydney Cricket Ground at right. To the top right of the SCG is the Sydney Showground. A speedway track that closed in 1994, the Sydney Showground was also the site of the Sydney Royal Easter Show from 1882 until 1997 when it was leased by Fox Studios Australia. *Craig Lamotte/Corbis 42-18358137*

ABOVE: Sun sets over the SCG during a Twenty20 match between Australia and England on 9 January 2007. Five light towers were built in 1978 to allow day/night fixtures. *Philip Brown/Corbis 42-17763135*

RIGHT: As the West Indies play Australia, the scores are displayed on the new electronic board erected above The Hill after the old concrete scoreboard was closed in 1983. *John Carnemolla/Corbis 42-17985273*

LEFT: This aerial view of the SCG dated 4 January 1998 shows a packed house during the Second Test against South Africa. Shane Warne demolished South Africa, taking 11–109 as Australia won by an innings. *Stephen Munday /Allsport/Getty Images 1924475*

RIGHT: As the Australian team makes its way out of the Members' Pavilion onto the field, Kevin Pietersen of England comes out to resume his innings at the start of day four of the fifth test, 5 January 2007. He made 29 and England lost by 10 wickets. The green-roofed buildings are the Members Pavilion and Ladies Stand further on. There is currently a 10-year waiting list to become a member. *John Pryke/Getty Images 72928766*

ENGLAND

BIRMINGHAM—EDGBASTON CRICKET GROUND

EDGBASTON CRICKET GROUND

Address: Edgbaston Road, Edgbaston, Birmingham,
West Midlands, B5 7QU
Website: www.visitus.edgbaston.com/ground
Capacity: 21,000
Opening date: June 1886

Memorable moments:

1902 First test, England v Australia, played 29–31 May.
W. Rhodes has figures of 11-3-17-7 as Australia
slump to 36 all out. The 3-day match is drawn
1924 South Africa out for ground's lowest score of 30
(A.E.R. Gilligan 6.3-4-7-6)
1957 P.B.H. May (285*) and M.C. Cowdrey (154) put
on 411, a ground record, to save the match
against the West Indies
1963 Chasing 309 to win, F.S. Trueman takes 7–44 as
the West Indies are bowled out for 91, levelling
the series at 1–1
1972 First ODI, England v Australia, played on
28 August
1979 England score 633–5d against India (G. Boycott
155, D.I. Gower 200*) the ground's highest test
total
1981 I.T. Botham took 5–11 in Australia's second
innings during the Fourth Test
1994 B.C. Lara scores a world record 501* for
Warwickshire against Durham
1995 England (407 and 182) beat Australia (308 and
279) in a nailbiter as Australia's last two wickets
put on 45 and 59 and fall just three runs short
1999 World Cup semi-final between Australia and
South Africa ends tied on 213 as A.A. Donald is
run out on the last ball; Australia go through

Home to Warwickshire County Cricket Club, Edgbaston became a venue for test cricket in 1902 which heralded its emergence from rather basic beginnings. Only being used for four tests up to the late 1920s hardly established the ground as a major international cricketing arena, and it was not until the 1950s that it achieved a degree of permanency on the Test circuit. Of course, by then Edgbaston had emerged as a modern stadium, the City end of the ground now graced by the famous Thwaite Memorial Scoreboard.

Further development did not take place until the 1990s when the input of lottery money allowed the Eric Hollies Stand, the Edgbaston Cricket Centre and a cricket shop to be added to established structures like the R.E.S Wyatt, William Ansell and Raglan Stands. In 2005 discussions were afoot with regard to the possibility of the County Cricket Club joining Birmingham Football Club at a new stadium which would house 50,000 all-seated spectators. This ground-sharing scheme has since been replaced by a £30m, cricket-only redevelopment scheme that will include a new stand and increase the ground's capacity by 4,000.

The new scheme is good news for cricket lovers who, in the recent past, have witnessed some amazing events at the old ground. These include Brian Lara's world-record 501 not out for Warwickshire against Durham in 1994, Nick Knight's 255 for the county versus Sussex in 2002, the 1999 tied World Cup semi final between South Africa and Australia and England's two run victory over Australia during the 2005 Ashes series. For the Lara performance and the England victory alone, Edgbaston deserves a preservation order slapped upon it.

PREVIOUS PAGES: Day four of the First Test between England and South Africa at Lord's 13 July 2008. England were on top, the South Africans following on, but centuries by captain G.C. Smith (107), N.D. McKenzie (138) and H.M. Amla (104*) saved the game. The wonderful red-brick pavilion was built 1889–90 thanks to a loan from gin-millionaire William Nicholson who loaned £21,000. It has recently (2004–05) been restored to pristine condition. *Mike Hewitt/Getty Images 81920276*

RIGHT: A good crowd at Edgbaston on 4 August 2007 watches the Twenty20 Cup semifinal between Kent Spitfires and Sussex Sharks. *Tom Shaw/Getty Images 75963345*

FAR LEFT: Edgbaston during the ODI between England and the West Indies on 4 July 2007. The West Indies won thanks to an unbeaten century (116*) by Shiv Chanderpaul who took part in a ground's best ODI third-wicket partnership with M.N. Samuels (77). *Getty Images for NatWest) 75027210*

LEFT: Aerial view of Edgbaston during the 21 May 1993 ODI between England and Australia. England scored a respectable 277–5 (R.A. Smith 167*) but Australia chased the runs down to win with nine balls remaining (M.E. Waugh 113, A.R. Border 86*). *John Gichigi/Allsport 965527*

FOLLOWING PAGES:
LEFT: The 1950 Thwaite Memorial Scoreboard shows Warwickshire's highest ever total (810–4d), Brian Lara's world record 501*, and his partner K.J. Piper's 116 (made out of a Warwickshire-best fifth-wicket partnership of 322) during the County Championship match against Durham. *Shaun Botterill/Allsport 1270300*

RIGHT: A sparse crowd watches the Liverpool and Victoria County Championship Division One match between Warwickshire and Middlesex at Edgbaston on 16 June 2006. *Getty Images for ECB 71461755*

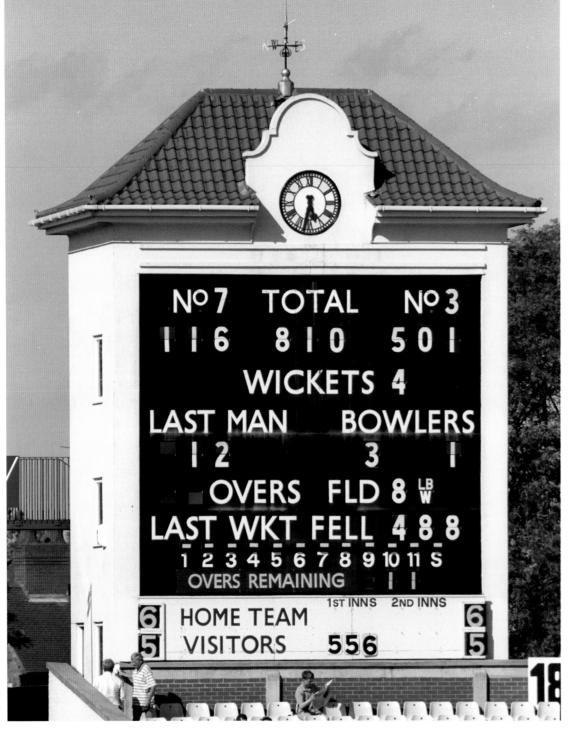

CHESTER-LE-STREET—RIVERSIDE

RIVERSIDE GROUND

Address: County Ground, Riverside, Chester-le-Street, Co. Durham, DH3 3QR
Website: www.durhamccc.co.uk
Capacity: 5,000 (17,000 for internationals)
Opening Date: 1995

Memorable moments:

1999 First ODI, Pakistan v Scotland, played on 20 May. Pakistan win by 94 runs

2003 Riverside became the first new test venue in England in over 100 years when Zimbabwe were England's opponents. England bowler Richard Johnson took 6–33 in Zimbabwe's first innings helping to dismiss them for what is still the ground's lowest test total of 94

2005 England compile the ground's top test innings total of 447–3d (M.E. Trescothick 151, I.R. Bell 162*—ground's highest individual score) against Bangladesh

2007 England beat the West Indies by seven wickets thanks to a first innings knock of 128 by Durham's own Paul Collingwood and Monty Panesar's 5–46 in the visitors' second innings

2008 First T20I, England v South Africa, due to be played on 20 August falls foul of the English summer weather and is abandoned without a ball being bowled

Durham County Cricket Club and its home ground have come a long way since the club was granted first-class status in 1991. Prior to this momentous event, Durham had existed as a minor county since 1882.

By 1995 the Chester-le-Street venue was ready to see action with its two pavilions and County Stand in place and areas for temporary stands indicating future ambitions. These temporary stands are used for international matches. The facilities for wheelchair access and the numbers of disabled toilets put more established grounds to shame. All this had become possible through the help of the local and county councils whose enthusiasm had been partly generated by funds from such as the Sports Council and the Forestry Commission. The Riverside is only part of an area which contains other benefits for sports enthusiasts.

This forward-thinking attitude bore fruit when, in 1999, two World Cup matches were awarded. Test cricket could not be far away and in 2003 the Riverside hosted the Second Test between England and Zimbabwe, a crushing win for the home side by an innings and 69 runs.

Subsequently, the north-east has seen a further test when England beat Bangladesh (another innings victory for the hosts) and two one-day internationals when England found both New Zealand and Australia too strong for them.

With question marks hanging over more-established test venues, the future for the Riverside is looking decidedly rosy.

RIGHT: England and Australia play a day/night ODI on 23 June 2005. After scoring 266 (A. Symonds 73, D.R. Martyn 68*) the visitors reduced England to 6–3 and the home side could only make 209. In September 2008 Durham CC unveiled plans for installation of permanent (those shown are temporary) floodlights and improvements to the seating to raise the capacity to 20,000. *Ian Hodgson/Reuters/Corbis 42-15468597*

LEEDS—HEADINGLEY CARNEGIE STADIUM

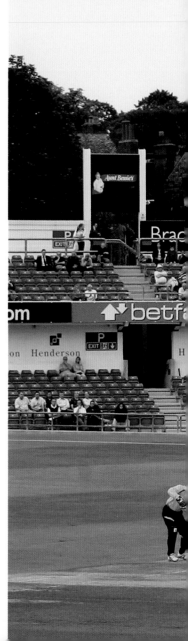

HEADINGLEY CARNEGIE STADIUM

Address: Cricket Ground, St. Michael's Lane, Leeds, West Yorkshire, LS6 3BU
Website: www.yorkshireccc.org.uk
Capacity: 14,000
Opening date: 1899

Memorable moments:

1899   First Test, England v Australia, played between 29 June and 1 July. Rain wipes out the third (and final) day leaving England needing 158 for victory with all second innings wickets intact

1930   D.G. Bradman scores 334 (then a world record) of which 309 come in a day

1934   D.G. Bradman scores 304 and puts on a ground record 388 for the fourth wicket with W.H. Ponsford (181)

1965   J.H. Edrich scores 311 against New Zealand and puts on a ground record 369 for the second wicket with K.F. Barrington (163)

1973   First ODI, England v West Indies, played on 5 September

1977   G. Boycott scored his 100th hundred (total 191) in the Fourth Test of the Ashes series.

1981   England follow on 227 runs behind Australia and are 135 for 7 in their second innings before I.T. Botham's 149* and R.G.D. (8–43) take them to victory

1993   Ground highest test innings total by Australia of 653–4d (D.C. Boon 107, A.R. Border 200*, S.R. Waugh 157*). Border and Waugh also put on 332*, a ground record for the fifth wicket)

2000   West Indies bowled out for ground's lowest test total of 61 (A.R. Caddick 5–14)

Home to Yorkshire County Cricket Club, Headingley witnessed its first test match in the year it opened when England and Australia drew.

The layout of the ground includes the North Stand at the Kirkstall Lane End, the uncovered West Stand where the scoreboard and Dickie Bird clock are situated, plus the ageing grandstand. Uniquely, the pavilion, tucked away in a corner of the ground, does not house the dressing rooms, which are located at the side of the pitch.

Late in 2005, for the first time in their history, YCCC acquired ownership of their own ground after a tie-up with Leeds Metropolitan University and a loan from Leeds City Council. In future the ground will be called the Headingley Carnegie Stadium, thanks to a huge redevelopment involving Leeds Rhinos rugby league team and their rugby union counterparts the Tykes. One of the larger proposals is to build a stand which will serve both cricket and rugby grounds

Until these latest moves, the future of Headingley as a Test Match venue was in doubt—but with the impending major surgery at both ends of the ground it seems international cricket will remain for some time to come.

It is unthinkable that a ground that has witnessed such events as two triple centuries from Don Bradman, John Edrich's triple in 1965, Boycott's achievement before his own crowd and the epic 1981 Ashes test, when Botham and Willis contrived to snatch victory from nowhere, should be relegated to non-international status.

RIGHT: The electronic scoreboard shows the details as Gordon Muchall and Gary Pratt of Durham bat during the Twenty20 match between Yorkshire and Durham at Headingley Carnegie Stadium on 27 June 2006. *Paul Gilham/Getty Images 71307473*

LEFT: 21 July 1981: one of the great days of English cricket. Ian Botham hits a four during his innings of 149* in the Third Ashes Test. As every England supporter knows, 500–1 odds were given by Ladbrooks who had to pay out after England's inspired 18-run fightback victory. *Adrian Murrell/Allsport 1270560*

RIGHT: Rainclouds gather over a good Headingley crowd during play in the Twenty20 Cup between Yorkshire Phoenix and Lancashire Lightning on 14 July 2004. There's no doubt that the introduction of Twenty20 has invigorated spectators. *Laurence Griffiths/Getty Images 51058983*

ABOVE: Headingley has been called the Headingley Carnegie Stadium since 2006 sponsorship by the sports faculty of Leeds Metropolitan University. A ground not known for its pavilion or covered stands needs a makeover to keep test cricket and there are many plans under review, including one to build the Headingley Carnegie Pavilion. This view shows action during the Frizell County Championship game between Yorkshire and Lancashire on 21 July 2002. *Laurence Griffiths/Getty Images 82017405*

RIGHT: The ground on 27 May 1996 during the second ODI between England and India. A low-scoring game was won by England by six wickets. The church spire belongs to St. Michael's. *Adrian Murrell/Allsport UK 1580076*

LONDON—LORD'S CRICKET GROUND

LORD'S CRICKET GROUND

Address:
Lord's Cricket Ground, St John's Wood, London NW8 8QN
Website: www.lords.org
Capacity: 30,000
Opening date: 1814

Memorable moments:

1787 Thomas Lord opened his first ground in Dorset Fields and the MCC was formed.

1884 First test, England v Australia, played 21–23 July

1890 Present Pavilion built. (Architect: Thomas Verity.)

1923 W.G. Grace Memorial Gates erected in St John's Wood Road (Architect: Sir Herbert Baker).

1930 729–6d Australia's total is ground's highest test score (D.G. Bradman 254, W.M. Woodfull 155)

1947 W.J. Edrich (189), D.C.S. Compton (208) put on ground record 370 for third wicket

1966 G. Sobers (163*) and D.A.J. Holford (105*) break English hearts with an unbeaten 274* game-saving partnership for the sixth wicket after having been effectively 10–5 in their second innings

1972 First ODI, England v Australia, played on 26 August

1974 India all out for 42 (C.M. Old 5-21) ground's lowest test total

1975 England score 334-4 (Amiss 137) in World Cup ODI against India

1980 Centenary Test Match, England v Australia

1990 Graham Gooch made 333 (still the ground's top score) and 123 in England's victory over India

1999 World Cup Final. Australia brush aside Pakistan to win by eight wickets

When Thomas Lord eventually established the ground named after him, he could scarcely have realised that, close to two hundred years later, Lord's would still be regarded as both the headquarters of the game and most revered of cricketing venues. That a structure built in the same century as the ground's opening would still take centre stage would also have been unimaginable. The structure concerned is, of course, the pavilion. Built in 1890, it is flanked on one side by the Warner Stand dating from 1958 and, on the other, by the less imposing Allen Stand.

At the opposite end, referred to as the Nursery, are the Compton and Edrich Stands, at the back of which is a second pitch used on an annual basis for such events as the women's Varsity match.

To the sides of the main pitch, the grandstand built in 1997 to replace its seventy-year-old predecessor designed by Sir Herbert Baker looms large.

Across the pitch sits the Mound Stand, completed in 1987, and the Tavern, built twenty years earlier. The standing area in front of the Tavern was, for a considerable time, a hotbed for serious but controlled drinking and genuinely original ribaldry which added to the atmosphere on big match days. Sadly, with an increase in irresponsible behaviour, this part of the ground had to be re-vamped.

Lord's Cricket Ground is the home ground of Middlesex and is privately owned by the Marylebone Cricket Club (MCC): to play there is still every cricketer's dream.

RIGHT: Lord's had never seen a day/night fixture before the NatWest Pro 40 match between Middlesex and Derbyshire on 10 September 2007. Artificial lights were set up for the game that resulted in a four-wicket win for the home team. It was definitely a sign of times to come. This view from the Nursery End shows two of the lights on either side of the pavilion.
Philip Brown/Corbis 42-19068488

LEFT: Another 13 July 2008 view of Lord's, this one from the from the Edrich Stand. It is named after Middlesex and England stalwart W.J. Edrich, whose friend and compatriot D.C.S. Compton is similarly honoured in the name of the stand on the other side of the Media Centre. In 1947 Middlesex won 19 of 26 County Championship matches and were the best team in England. Compton scored 3,816 runs in the season, averaging 90.85 with 18 centuries (including four against the touring Springboks); Edrich scored 3,539 at 80.43 with 12 centuries (two against South Africa). *Mike Hewitt/ Getty Images 81920216*

ABOVE: A view from the Warner Stand across to the Media Centre and Edrich Stand during the fourth day of the season's opener between MCC and county champions Sussex on 16 April 2007. The Mound Stand, on the right, was designed by architect Michael Hopkins and built in the late 1980s. Its original signature tented roof was replaced in 2006 by a similar version made from more advanced materials. *Clive Rose/Getty Images 73896137*

RIGHT: A closeup of the innovative Media Centre designed by Future Systems Limited to house 250 journalists. It was the first all-aluminium, semi-monocoque building in the world. Opened in time for the 1999 World Cup, it won the prestigious RIBA Stirling prize. *Construction Photography/Corbis 42-18380121*

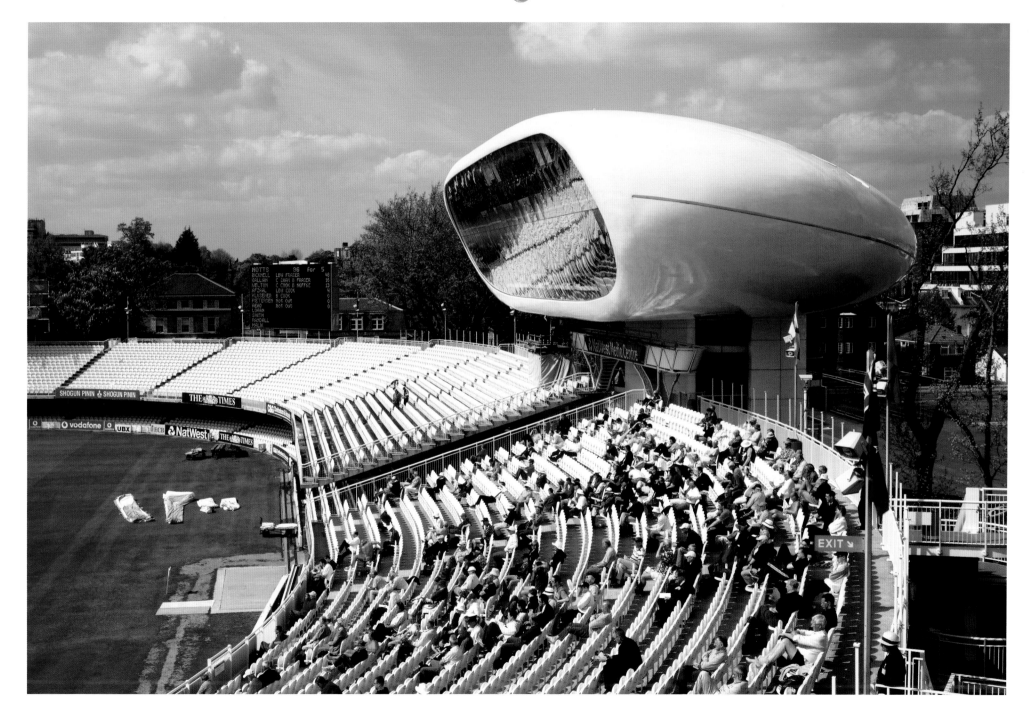

LEFT: Presented to the club in 1925 and designed by Sir Herbert Baker, the iconic Father Time weathervane was originally positioned on the northwestern stand until that was demolished to make way for the new Grand Stand (see below). At present Father Time can be seen between the Mound and Tavern stands. *Mike Hewitt/Getty Images 81914671*

RIGHT: A May 2007 view of the new Grand Stand that was completed in June 1998. Architects Nicholas Grimshaw & Partners designed a roof suspended by hangers from a central mast covering two tiers that allowed an increase in seating from 4,000 to over 6,000. The threatening skies in the picture would lead to interruptions for bad light and rain throughout the drawn match. *Tommy Hindley/ NewSport/Corbis 42-18400253*

LONDON—KENNINGTON OVAL

KENNINGTON OVAL

Address: The Oval Cricket Ground, Kennington, London SE11 5SS
Website: www.surreycricket.com
Capacity: 23,500
Opening Date: 1845

Memorable moments:

1872 First F.A. Cup Final is played at the Oval. Wanderers beat the Royal Engineers 1–0

1880 The first ever Test match between England and Australia on 6 September. England beat Australia by five wickets

1882 The Ashes are born after England, chasing only 85 to win, slump from 51 for 2 to 78 all out. The next morning *The Sporting Times* published its famous mock obituary and the legend was born

1896 Ground's lowest test total of 44 by Australia (R. Peel 6–23)

1934 W.H. Ponsford (266) and D.G. Bradman (244) put on 451 for the second wicket, still a ground record

1938 England beat Australia by an innings and 579 runs, after amassing a total of 903–7d (L. Hutton 364, a Test record at the time; M. Leyland 187, J. Hardstaff Jr 169*).

1948 Australia win by an innings and 149 in D.G. Bradman's last test. England 52 and 188; Australia 389 (Bradman b W.E. Hollies 0; A.R. Morris 196. Next highest score was Hutton's 64)

1973 First ODI, England v West Indies played on 7 September

2007 First T20I, England v West Indies, played on 28 June

Leased from the Duchy of Cornwall, the Oval has been the home of Surrey County Cricket Club since 1845 when a pitch was laid consisting of turf from Tooting Common. It did not have a pavilion until 1858, and this had to serve the club for 40 years before another took shape.

Apart from the pavilion, the Vauxhall Stand supplied the only covered area for some considerable time, the Oval not being the most spectator-friendly of grounds. It could have been argued that the gasometers that loom on the eastern side of the ground had more presence than the ground itself. Welcome additions arrived in the 1980s, when three new stands were constructed, named after Surrey stalwarts Bedser, Lock and Laker.

In 1988 the first of a series of sponsorship deals were struck, the ground being renamed the Foster's Oval; in recent times it has changed to the AMP Oval and, latterly, to the Brit Oval.

In eighteen months from February 2004 the Vauxhall End of the ground witnessed the much-needed construction of the OCS Stand costing £25 million, thus increasing the capacity to its current figure. This addition contains four floors, housing two banqueting suites with views of the ground, a media centre, sports hall and conference facilities.

With these improvements and a deal struck with the ECB, the Oval is guaranteed one-day internationals and test matches for many years to come.

RIGHT: View from the Vauxhall End during the International Twenty20 match between England and the West Indies on 29 June 2007. The Members' Pavilion was completed in 1898; to the left of the photograph is the Laker Stand (named after Surrey and England's most famous off spinner Jim Laker, whose record haul of 19–90 against Australia in 1956 is still easily the best individual bowling analysis). On the other side is the Bedser Stand (named for Alec, the younger brother of twin Eric: Surrey stalwart, test selector and mean fast bowler). *Getty Images for NatWest 74957832*

Left: Aerial view of the Oval looking over the new OCS Stand, from the Vauxhall End on 25 March 2008. The older Vauxhall End Surridge, Fender, Jardine and Peter May North stands were redeveloped from the end of the 2002 season and replaced by the fantastic four-tier OCS Stand, which opened in May 2005. *Jason Hawkes/Getty Images 80632142*

Following pages:

Left: The famous gasometers that overlook the Oval are in fact younger than the ground by eight years, having been erected in 1853. They are under threat of redevelopment, although it is likely they will remain as part of the Oval's heritage. This 1995 photograph shows the ground before the recent redevelopment. *Mike King/Corbis KN001089*

Right: Another aerial view of the Oval, taken on 14 January 2007, shows off the OCS Stand. Note the proximity of the gasometers and, on the river directly above them the Art Deco style SIS (MI6) building designed by Terry Farrell and built by John Laing. *Jason Hawkes/Corbis 42-18944651*

OLD TRAFFORD

Address: Old Trafford Cricket Ground, Talbot Road, Manchester, M16 OPX
Website: www.lccc.co.uk
Capacity: 19,000
Opening Date: 1857

Memorable moments:

1884   First test, England v Australia, played on 10–12 July

1912   Australian Jimmy Matthews performed the unique feat of a hat-trick in both innings in a game against South Africa

1952   India all out for ground's lowest test score 58 (F.S. Trueman 8–31)

1956   On an old-fashioned 'sticky wicket', J.C. Laker produces world's best bowling figures of 19–90

1964   Australia scored ground's highest test total of 656–8d (R.B. Simpson 311, W.M. Lawry 106) England reply with 611 (K.F. Barrington 256, E.R. Dexter 174) still top individual scores

1972   First ODI, England v Australia, on 24 August

1995   Dominic Cork ensured anyone having a Sunday morning snooze was rudely woken with one of most dramatic opening overs ever seen, as he took his hat-trick against West Indies. He took 7–43 in the second innings, the best figures by an Englishman on debut

2008   First T20I, England v New Zealand, played on 13 June

In the ten years before Lancashire County Cricket Club arrived at Old Trafford they had two previous homes. Nearly 150 years on, a debate is still taking place as to the future of both club and venue, much of it due to the requirement to update the famous old ground. The necessity for work to be carried out on the pavilion and the demolition of other stands a couple of years ago masked more pressing needs.

It has been remarked that the ground has a pre-war feel to it, but vthat feeling will be dispelled when the ground's redevelopment is completed. The stadium stands separately from the football ground of the same name and could do with some of the cash that has been lavished on the home of Manchester United. Pop music concerts have recently been a feature at the venue, bringing in much-needed revenue.

Test matches have been played at Old Trafford since 1884, none more breathtaking than the 1956 fourth Ashes test when England's Jim Laker spun the home side to victory. In Australia's first innings, he returned figures of 9 for 37 and followed it up with 10 for 53 in the second. Unsurprisingly, these combined bowling figures have never been bettered in international cricket.

In terms of drama packed into the first over of the day, little could top Dominic Cork's Sunday morning charge as he bagged a hat-trick against the West Indies in 1995.

RIGHT: The Members' Pavilion during day five of the Third npower Test between England and the West Indies on 11 June 2007. England won by 60 runs bowling out the visitors for 394 chasing 455. Preliminary work on redevelopment started on 23 August 2008 and the ground was closed for the rest of the season. The stadium will be opened during the 2009 season, although the work will continue for some time. *Julian Herbert/Getty Images 74539148*

LEFT: Dark clouds form over the pavilion during day one of the Third npower Test between England and the West Indies on 12 August 2004. The bad luck was with the visitors, who lost a cracking test match by seven wickets as England chased 231. The West Indies had collapsed from 95–2 to 165 all out in their second innings thanks to some excellent pace bowling by Harmison (4–44) and Flintoff (3–26). *Laurence Griffiths/Getty Images 72481011*

FOLLOWING PAGES:
LEFT: England take on India in a floodlit ODI on 30 August 2007. England successfully chased 212 to win by three wickets with 12 balls remaining. *Paul Ellis/AFP/Getty Images 76430784*

RIGHT: Old Trafford during the Third Test between England and Australia on 7 July 1997. Australia won the match by 268 runs and the series 3–2. *Adrian Murrell/Allsport 1621467*

NOTTINGHAM—TRENT BRIDGE

TRENT BRIDGE

Address: Trent Bridge, Nottingham, Nottinghamshire,
NG2 6AG
Website: www.trentbridge.co.uk
Capacity: 15,350
Opening Date: 1841

Memorable moments:
1899 Ground's first test, England v Australia, 1–3 June
1938 England score 658–8d (E. Paynter 216, C.J.
       Barnett 126, D.C.S. Compton 102, L. Hutton
       100)—the ground's top test total. Australia
       answer with 411 (S.J. McCabe 232) and, following
       on, 427–6 (D.G. Bradman 144*, W.A. Brown 133)
       to draw the game
1954 During the Pakistan game, D.C.S. Compton put
       on 192 in 105 minutes in partnership with
       Trevor Bailey as he powered his way to his, and
       the ground's, highest test score of 278.
1960 South Africa all out for 88 (Trueman 5–27), still
       the ground's lowest test score
1974 First ODI, England v Pakistan, played on 31
       August
1977 G. Boycott returning to test cricket after three
       years out of the team, and A.P.E. Knott put on
       215 for the sixth wicket in the first innings and
       England beat Australia by 7 wickets. I.T. Botham
       takes 5–74 in the first innings of his debut test
1989 G.R. Marsh (138) and M.A. Taylor (219) put on
       329 for the first wicket batting unbeaten through
       first day of test for 301*
2006 M. Muralitharan takes 8–70 in the second innings
       as Sri Lanka beat England by 134 runs and draw
       the three-match series 1–1

Although officially established in 1841, records show that cricket had been played in the immediate Trent Bridge vicinity during the previous decade. From the 1860s, Nottinghamshire County Cricket Club shared the facilities with Notts County Football Club, who did not move on until 1910; it was then felt that, with test cricket having been introduced to the ground in 1899, the two sports could no longer co-habit.

Even though the ground has seen many changes over the decades, at its heart sits the famous pavilion which has retained its essential architectural elements since erection in 1886.

This historic structure contrasts dramatically with the Radcliffe Road Stand built at the north end in 1998. This incorporates the cricket centre made up of the press box, a lecture theatre, hospitality boxes and two indoor cricket schools which can be transformed for other purposes. On the eastern side sits the Fox Road Stand, basking in its 21st Century glory, whilst the William Clarke Stand, named after the ground's founder, can be found opposite.

In keeping with other cricket venues, the Trent Bridge authorities have realised that underused facilities are not an option in the modern world, so parties, conferences, corporate events and banquets are just some of the functions Trent Bridge is keen to cater for, and if anybody wants it the entire ground can be hired out. An historic venue with a modern attitude.

RIGHT: A view across the ground to the new West Wing Stand, on the Bridgford Road side. Work started on the development with its flower-like floodlights in 2007. It replaced the Parr Stand and old West Wing, and was was completed in time for a royal opening before the Third npower Test between England and New Zealand. This image was taken on the second day, 6 June 2008: England won by an innings and nine runs, Sidebottom taking 6–67 in the visitors' second innings. *Philip Brown/Corbis 42-20378827*

BANGALORE—M. CHINNASWAMY STADIUM

M. CHINNASWAMY STADIUM

Address: Karnataka State Cricket Association, Mahatma Gandhi Road, Bangalore - 560001
Website: www.cricketkarnataka.com
Capacity: 55,000
Opening Date: 1972

Memorable moments:

1974 First test, played against West Indies, ends in loss for the home team

1982 First ODI, India beat Sri Lanka

1987 Pakistan win by 16 runs after having been dismissed for 116, the lowest test total on the ground, in their first innings. India fall short in spite of 96 by S.M. Gavaskar. Pakistan bowlers Iqbal Qasim (67-26-121-9) and Tauseef Ahmed (72.5-19-139-9) do the damage with only 18 overs bowled by other bowlers

1996 World Cup quarter-final ODI sees India defeat Pakistan by 39 runs (but lose in the semis to Sri Lanka)

2004 Anil Kumble took his 400th test wicket when India faced Australia, on the ground where he had taken his 300th. Harbhajan Singh has best bowling match analysis of 71.1-12-224-11 but still ends op on the losing side

2005 The ground's top individual test score (267) is made by Younis Khan who puts on 324 for the second wicket with Inzamam-ul-Haq (184)

2007 India score 626 against Pakistan, the highest test score on the ground, with centuries from S.C. Ganguly (239), Yuvraj Singh (169) and I.K. Pathan (102)

This venue is named after the former president of the Indian Cricket Board, who spent many dedicated years in local cricket administration. Building began in 1970 and first-class cricket was being played at the ground two years later.

The first test match at the Chinnaswamy was played against the West Indies in 1974 when Viv Richards and Gordon Greenidge made their debuts. The ground is situated right in the heart of the city, between the Mahatma Gandhi Road and a park.

The modern pavilion stands at the southern end of the ground, which apart from the three-tier President's Stand to its left, gives way to a single two-tier stand which sweeps around the rest of the ground. To the north-east a large score-board and floodlights, installed for the 1996 World Cup, serve the stadium. Members are well catered for, having access to badminton courts, a swimming pool and a gymnasium. The National Cricket Academy houses its indoor training facilities at the Chinnaswamy.

India's fortunes in Bangalore have fluctuated over thirty-plus years; in recent times the results, in test matches at least, have gone against them.

Heavy defeats were suffered at the hands of South Africa, Australia and most recently Pakistan in 2005 by 168 runs. The home team's best ever result came in 1977 when, although 3–0 down in the series, a 177-run victory over England at least salvaged some pride.

PREVIOUS PAGES: The Brabourne Stadium where England warmed up against a Mumbai XI during the winter tour of India on 11 November 2008. The Brabourne Stadium hasn't hosted a test match since 1973, and had been allocated a game in 2008 during England's tour. The terrorist attacks put paid to that and we can only look forward to its re-entry into test cricket in the future. *Julian Herbert/Getty Images 83641057*

RIGHT: A view of the ground during day four of the First Test between India and Australia on 12 October 2008. Australia would draw the match but lose the series 2–0. *Global Cricket Ventures/BCCI via Getty Images 83235654*

LEFT: The Australian cricket team training at the M.Chinnaswamy Stadium on 7 October 2008. The Board of Control for Cricket in India (BCCI) chose Bangalore as the location for the National Cricket Academy in 2000, and one reason is that it has a fine stadium with strong day/night facilities. There are plans to increase the seating capacity to 70,000.
Michael Steele/Getty Images 83154508

RIGHT: Another view of play during the First Test between India and Australia in October 2008, giving a good impression of the size of the stands.
Michael Steele/Getty Images 83227383

CHENNAI—M.A. CHIDAMBARAM STADIUM

M. A. CHIDAMBARAM STADIUM

Address: Chepauk, Chennai, India
Capacity: 50,000
Opening Date: 1934

Memorable moments:

1934 First test, a loss to England by 202 runs. H. Verity takes 7–49 and 4–104

1952 India's first ever test win—against England by an innings and 8 runs. M.H. Mankad takes 8–55 and 4–53; centuries for P. Roy (111) and P.R. Umrigar (130*)

1983 S.M. Gavaskar makes his highest test score (236*) in a draw against the West Indies

1986 The tied test between India and Australia as India chasing 348 lose Maninder Singh lbw to G.R.J. Matthews. In this match S.M. Gavaskar became the first player to make 100 consecutive test appearances

1987 First ODI: Australia (270) beat India (269) by one run, dismissing Maninder Singh with the penultimate ball

2001 India beat Australia by two wickets chasing 155, losing six wickets for 50 runs after having been 101–2

2008 V. Sehwag makes the highest individual test score on the ground, 319 with 5 sixes and 42 fours off 304 balls

2008 India beat England by six wickets, scoring 387 in the fourth innings thanks to a masterful 103* by Sachin Tendulkar who is well-supported in an unbeaten fifth wicket stand of 163 by Yuvraj Singh (85*)

Formerly known as the Chepauk Stadium, the MAC has become synonymous with sporting, appreciative crowds and pitches that give both batsman and bowler a chance. It is not uncommon for the home supporters to vigorously applaud the achievements of visiting individuals or teams.

At the southern end can be found both the Madras Cricket Club Pavilion and the Anna Pavilion which are directly opposite the Royal Sundaram and United India Insurance Stands, close to the V. Pattabhiraman Gate and electronic scoreboard. To the east and west are further stands and popular enclosures.

India's first test win over England was achieved in 1952 but, after a further game against Pakistan later that year, the MAC disappeared into the international wilderness until the visit of the West Indies in 1967. No such hiatus has occurred since, with Chennai becoming a regular stop-off on the circuit.

Apart from the epic tied test, other highlights include Sunil Gavaskar recording his 30th Test century in December 1983, Vinoo Mankad taking 8 for 55 in that initial victory in 1952, debutante leg-spinner Narendra Hirwani mesmerising the West Indians in a 1988 win when he took 16 wickets for 136 runs, and Gundappa Viswanath making the England bowlers toil in achieving a double-hundred in 1982.

RIGHT: Day three of the First Test between India and England on 13 December 2008 saw the visitors in the driving seat as they closed on 172–3 in 54.0 overs (A.J. Strauss 73, P.D. Collingwood 60)—247 runs ahead with seven wickets in hand. *Global Cricket Ventures/BCCI via Getty Images 84018220*

DELHI—FEROZ SHAH KOTLA

FEROZ SHAH KOTLA

Address: Delhi District Cricket Association, Feroz Shah Kotla Ground, Bahadur Shah Zafar Marg, New Delhi - 110002
Capacity: c45,000 when reconstruction is finished
Opening Date: 1883

Memorable moments:

1948 First test on the ground was a draw with the West Indies who made 631 in their innings (C.L. Walcott 152, E.D. Weekes 128, R.J. Christiani 107 and G.E. Gomez 101)

1955 B. Sutcliffe of New Zealand makes the highest individual test score on the ground (230*)

1959 West Indies makes highest test total on the ground 644–8d (J.K.C. Holt 123, O.G. Smith 100, J.S. Solomon 100*)

1969 India defeated Australia thanks to Bishan Bedi and Erapalli Prasanna taking nine wickets apiece

1982 India won first ODI chasing 278 and winning easily by six wickets with nearly ten overs left (K. Srikkanth 95)

1987 Staged the World Cup game between India and Australia. India won by 56 runs but Australia eventually took the trophy

1998 R.T. Ponting makes the highest ODI score on the ground (145) against Zimbabwe

1999 India beat Pakistan by 212 runs with Kumble taking all ten wickets (26.3-9-74-10) in the second innings to add to the four he took in the first

The Kotla recently underwent a reconstruction programme which vastly overran and left the local cricket authorities with major games to play without a finished stadium worthy of the name to hold them in. The latest round of changes to the old ground involved demolishing the whole ground, bar the pavilion, and towards the end of 2005 much work still had to be completed.

The ground's test record started in November 1948 when the visiting West Indies amassed a score of over 600 (four batsman scoring centuries) but India still managed to squeeze out a draw. Four years later Pakistan were defeated by an innings to give the home side a first win at the venue.

Thereafter the Kotla failed to become a place of celebration –India only tasted victory twice out of nineteen games played up until their 1993 win over Zimbabwe. Happier times were to come, however, for the Zimbabwe game, which featured a double-century from Vinod Kambli and heralded a run of five victories, including the toppling of both Australia and Pakistan.

The latter win, always satisfactory for home fans, was doubly sweet for Anil Kumble who, after taking four wickets in Pakistan's first innings, took all ten in the second when it looked possible that the visitors were on their way to a winning target. Kumble entered the record books as only the second man to take all ten wickets in a test innings, England's Jim Laker being the first.

RIGHT: After beating Australia by 320 runs at Mohali, Chandigarh, India had the better of the draw on a batsman's track in New Delhi. This is a view of play during day four of the Third Test on 1 November 2008. *Global Cricket Ventures/BCCI via Getty Images 83523783*

KOLKATA—EDEN GARDENS

EDEN GARDENS

Address: The Cricket Association of Bengal, Dr B.C. Roy Club House, Eden Gardens, Kolkata 700021
Capacity: 90,000–100,000
Opening Date: 1864

Memorable moments:

1934 First test, against England, is drawn

1962 India claims its first test victory at Eden Gardens after a 27-year wait bowling out England for 233 to win by 187 runs

1978 West Indies hold on for a draw as they collapse to 197–9 chasing 335 on the fifth day after S.M. Gavaskar (182*) and D.B. Vengsarkar (157*) put on a ground record unbroken second-wicket partnership of 344*

1987 The first ODI on the ground sees Pakistan beat India by two wickets with three balls remaining after chasing 239, thanks to Saleem Malik's unbeaten 72 from 36 balls with a six and 11 fours

1996 Lance Klusener takes 8–64, the best test bowling figures on the ground, and Gary Kirsten scores centuries in both innings (102 and 133) as South Africa beat India by 329 runs. The first-wicket partnership of 236 (A.C. Hudson 146, G. Kirsten 102) is still a ground test record.

2001 V.V.S. Laxman (281) and R.S. Dravid (180) put on 376 as India, following on, total 657–7d in their second innings (the ground's top test innings total) and then bowl out Australia for 212 (Harbhajan Singh 6–73) in a famous 171-run victory

The Eden Gardens cricket ground is to India what Lord's is to England and the MCG Australia. This is a huge venue that sprung from recreational land presented to the people of Calcutta (Kolkata) by the governor-general back in the 19th Century. The influential Calcutta Cricket Club soon established itself at Eden Gardens and the first pavilion was built in 1871. First-class cricket had been played for less than twenty years when India entertained Douglas Jardine's team in January 1934 for Calcutta's first test. It would be another fourteen years before Eden Gardens would encounter another touring team and until 1961 before local cricket fans could celebrate a test victory, England the victims.

Little documentation is available regarding improvements to this vast arena, until the 1987 World Cup, when covered stands were erected, the Dr C. B. Roy Clubhouse took over the southern end of the ground and the pavilion was modernised. The Clubhouse is currently the headquarters of the Cricket Association of Bengal. In November 1993, the CAB celebrated its Diamond Jubilee and to mark the occasion, floodlights were installed for a one-day, day-night extravaganza involving five teams. Numerous stands are dotted around the ground with most of the upper tiers under cover, although the northern side is open to the elements.

Eden Gardens is an intimidating place for visiting players and supporters alike and even more so when home support gets totally out of control as it has in the past; a World Cup semi-final in 1996 had to be abandoned due to unruly crowd behaviour.

RIGHT: A capacity crowd at Eden Gardens during the TVS Triangular One Day Series Final between India and Australia on 18 November 2003. Australia won by 37 runs. *Shaun Botterill/Getty Images 2740189*

FOLLOWING PAGES:

LEFT: View of Eden Gardens during the first India v England ODI on 19 January 2002. India won this one by 22 runs, bowling England out for 259. The series was shared 3–3 after England won two tight games by two and five runs at the Feroz Shah Kotla, Delhi and Wankhede Stadium, Mumbai. *Tom Shaw/Getty Images 1080543*

RIGHT: Ever hopeful, spectators linger in the stands at Eden Gardens on 8 February 2007, as the ODI between India and Sri Lanka is halted by rain when Sri Lanka were 102–3. There was no more play. *Deshakalyan Chowhury/AFP/Getty Images 73255318*

MUMBAI—WANKHEDE STADIUM

WANKHEDE STADIUM

Address: Mumbai Cricket Association, Wankhede Stadium, D Road, Churchgate, Mumbai - 400020
Capacity: 45,000
Opening Date: 1974

Memorable moments:

1975 In the first test played on the ground, West Indian Clive Lloyd scores what is still the ground's highest individual total of 242* and puts on 250 for the sixth wicket with D.L. Murray (91)

1980 I.T. Botham's 7–48 is the best individual bowling performance on the ground until equalled by Harbhajan Singh in 2002

1986 D.B. Vengsarkar (164) and R.J. Shastri (121*) put on 298* for the sixth wicket against Australia

1987 Ground's first ODI, India v Sri Lanka, played on 17 January. In spite of being cut to 40 overs a side, the game sees the highest aggregate ODI score on the ground, India winning by 10 runs as Sri Lanka score 289–7 chasing 300. M. Azharuddin scores 108*

1993 India's Vinod Kambli scored 224 on his test debut against England, the ground's second highest test innings

2002 England win a thrilling ODI by five runs as India lose two wickets in the last over chasing 255

2004 Australia are bundled out for the ground's lowest test total of 93 while chasing 107 as India win by 13 runs, Harbhajan Singh taking 5–29

Mumbai (Bombay) had already seen test cricket played at two other venues before the Wankhede Stadium held its first international match in January 1975. This saw the West Indies amass over 600 runs in their first innings, crushing the home side thanks to a Clive Lloyd double-century.

In the short time the ground has staged international fixtures, the cricket has invariably been of the highest quality with Sunil Gavaskar in particular enjoying the batting track. He scored centuries in four successive tests, starting in 1976 against New Zealand and including 205 versus the West Indies.

Ian Botham was another who seemed to the relish playing in Mumbai; his century and 13 wickets in the Jubilee Test of 1980 was one of his best single-match hauls – and even though England lost the test the the following year, he still managed a nine-wicket total. Botham would definitely have approved when a few years later Ravi Shastri, playing on the same ground, hit six sixes in an over on his way to a fastest ever first-class double century.

The bowl that is Wankhede stands in a residential area containing high-rise flats and has been described as having basic facilities, even though it received a facelift for the 1995 World Cup. The Sunil Gavaskar Stand faces the Vithal Divecha Pavilion on the west side of the ground: the Sachin Tendulkar and Vijay Merchant stands are on the north side.

RIGHT: 15 November 2001—an England net session at the Wankhede Stadium which is undergoing renovation. They obviously didn't practice enough because they lost the series. *Tom Shaw/Allsport/ Getty Images 1061591*

LEFT: Ricky Ponting of Australia inspects the pitch on 5 November 2004—day three of the Fourth Test. Little does he know that by stumps India will have won the match when, chasing 107, his side falls for 93, Harbhajan Singh taking 5–29. *Hamish Blair/Getty Images 51676098*

RIGHT: The 1987 World Cup ODI semi-final was between hosts India and England. A century by Graham Gooch (115) and 4–52 by Eddie Hemmings won England a trip to Eden Gardens to face Australia. Australia won a thrilling final by nine runs. *Adrian Murrell/ Allsport 1270451*

LEFT: 7 November 2008—day two of the Fourth Test—is being played to a surprisingly thin crowd at the Cricket Association Stadium, Jamtha, Nagpur, the only test at that ground to date. India complete a first innings total of 441 and Australia end the day in a position of strength on 189–2. Over the next three days, however, India turn the tables and win by 172 runs. *Global Cricket Ventures/BCCI via Getty Images 83596868*

BELOW: The Jawaharlal Nehru Stadium at Kochi has only seen a handful of ODIs and has proved a batsman's track. India have won two-thirds of the games, but this 2007 ODI against Australia was an exception. Australia totalled 306–6 and India could only manage 222 in reply. *Hamish Blair/Getty Images 77149471*

NEW ZEALAND

AUCKLAND—EDEN PARK

EDEN PARK

Address: Auckland, New Zealand
Website: www.edenpark.co.nz
Capacity: 50,000
Opening Date: 1900

Memorable moments:

1930 First test—against England—sees two of the three days lost to rain and ends in a draw. K.S. Duleepsinhji (117) and E.H. Bowley (109) put on 111 for the second wicket

1933 Wally Hammond scores 336* out of 548, a world record at the time, scoring his runs in 318 minutes with 10 sixes and 34 fours

1955 England win by an innings as New Zealand make 26 in their second innings (Appleyard 6-3-7-4)

1956 New Zealand's first ever win in a test match when they defeat the West Indies by 190 runs.

1976 First ODI New Zealand defeat India by 80 runs

1976 E.A.S. Prasanna takes ground-best figures of 23-5-76-8 as India win by 8 wickets

1993 New Zealand beat Australia by 5 wickets; Shane Warne's first innings analysis is an abstemious 15-12-8-4

1999 Highest ground test total 621–5d scored by South Africa as D.J. Cullinan (275) and G. Kirsten (128) put on 183 for the third wicket

2000 Daniel Vettori takes match figures of 60-19-149-12 but can't stop Australia winning by 62 runs

2002 New Zealand recorded their first ever Auckland win over England, by 78 runs

2005 First T20I. Australia score 214 (R.T. Ponting 98 from 55 balls including 5 sixes and 8 fours) beating New Zealand by 44 runs

Eden Park came into existence at the turn of the 20th Century and established itself as a home for Auckland cricket in 1910 and rugby fifteen years later. Since the mid-1920s management has been in the hands of the Eden Park Trust Board who oversee all activities at the venue.

The oldest structure is the pavilion, constructed in the 1920s and a visible contrast to the contemporary feel of structures like the imposing ASB Bank Stand. All four main stands have both covered and uncovered seating.

Much has been made of the playing area shape which resembles a baseball diamond, leading to a marked imbalance in boundary distances from the wicket. The playing area was totally re-laid in 2003 without solving the problem but dealt with the constant worry that came with a major drainage headache. With New Zealand having won the honour to stage the 2011 Rugby World Cup, Eden Park can look forward to some major changes in the near future.

Since that first test win in 1956, when the West Indies were reduced to 77 all out in their second innings, New Zealand have had few victories to celebrate at Eden Park. Certainly, the Kiwis would rather forget the paltry 26 they were bowled out for against England in 1955. The two wins over Australia in the 1980s must still bring smiles to the faces of local fans, but in 2005 NZ were twice beaten comfortably by their closest rivals in Test and one-day confrontations.

PREVIOUS PAGES: Basin Reserve on 27 March 2004, the second day of the Third Test against South Africa. New Zealand finished their first innings on 297; South Africa had knocked off 273–3 by the close. *Touchline/Getty Images 3145637*

RIGHT: The fourth day of the Third Test continues under lights on 2 April 2002 at Eden Park. New Zealand declared on 269–9 at the end of the day and bowled England out for 233, 78 runs short. *Tom Shaw/Getty Images 1117622*

LEFT: Eden Park on 24 January 1997 during the first, drawn, test against England. England's innings of 521 was dominated by Surrey comrades A.J. Stewart (173) and G.P. Thorpe (119). *Graham Chadwick/Allsport/Getty Images 1255183*

ABOVE: New Zealand's Shane Bond celebrates after hitting the stump and winning the Twenty20I match against the West Indies. A tie had forced the bowl-off on 16 February 2006. *Phil Walter/Getty Images 56860497*

CHRISTCHURCH—AMI STADIUM

AMI STADIUM

Address: Christchurch, New Zealand
Website: www.jadestadium.co.nz
Capacity: 36,500
Opening Date: 1880

Memorable moments:

1930 In the first test on the ground—a win for England by 8 wickets—M.J.C. Allom took a hat-trick

1968 38 years after staging its first test, the Jade witnessed New Zealand's first victory, over India

1969 S.M. Nurse makes the highest score on the ground, 258 out of 417. 117* in 278 minutes by B.F. Hastings saves the draw for New Zealand

1971 Lowest ground total—65—by New Zealand against England who win by 8 wickets. D.L. Underwood figures 11.6-7-12-6 in first innings; 32.3-7-85-6 in the second

1973 First ODI results in a win for New Zealand by 22 runs against Pakistan

1987 West Indies win the fourth ODI of the season by 10 wickets, C.G. Greenidge (133*) and D.L. Haynes (53*) put on an unbroken 192 in just under 40 overs

1992 England make the highest total on the ground—580–9d (A.J. Stewart 148, R.A. Smith 96, A.J. Lamb 93) and win by an innings. P.C.R. Tufnell takes 11 wickets in the match including ground-best figures 46.1-25-47-7

2008 First T20I results in a win for England (193) by 50 runs

The first planned cricket match at what is now called the AMI Stadium, formerly known as Lancaster Park and Jade Stadium, was washed out. Consequently, Canterbury's debut at the ground took place in 1882 when they took on a representative England XI; official test cricket arrived in 1930 with a loss to England. Many other sports have been seen at the stadium, including trotting, cycling, athletics and currently rugby union. During World War II, the playing area was used for growing potatoes.

Since the 1950s when the embankment was enlarged, various projects have changed the face of the ground; two fresh stands were built in 1965, the Hadlee Stand was erected in 1995 and in 2000 the embankment plus the No 4 Stand disappeared, to be replaced by the DB Draught Stand and the enormous West Stand (Paul Kelly Motor Company Stand). Floodlighting, an innovation for New Zealand stadia, was installed in 1996.

Other structures of note are the No 1, No 2 and Smith City Stands. Rising above the DB can be found the scoreboard and the video replay screen. In keeping with other major NZ stadiums, the Jade will see further redevelopment before the 2011 Rugby World Cup, the stands on the eastern side being replaced by a single structure which will match the Western Stand in its grandeur.

Christchurch is home to the famous Hadlee family. Sir Richard, its most revered member and great all-rounder, performed wonderfully at his home ground, taking over 70 wickets at an average of just 21.51and averaging over 30 with the bat.

RIGHT: The sun sets during the fifth National Bank series ODI against England at the AMI Stadium on 23 February 2008. New Zealand won by 34 runs (D/L method). *Clive Rose/Getty Images 79951739*

LEFT: Australia's captain, Ricky Ponting, bats during day two of the First Test on 11 March 2005. He ended the day on 41* and Australia on 141–3 in reply to New Zealand's 433. In the background looms the Crusaders Super 12 rugby team's castle. *Hamish Blair/Getty Images 52372861*

RIGHT: The Jade Stadium on 13 February 2002 during the first ODI of the series against England. *Tom Shaw/Getty Images 1090832*

McLEAN PARK

Address: Napier, New Zealand
Capacity: 20,000
Opening Date: Its first test match in 1979, though sport has been played at this location for decades

Memorable moments:

1979 First test—against Pakistan—ends in a rain-affected draw

1983 First ODI game against Sri Lanka ends in victory by 7 wickets for New Zealand

1995 New Zealand all out for ground's lowest total, 109 (W.P.U.J.C. Vaas 5–47) in first innings, as Sri Lanka win by 241 runs

1997 The third ODI of the series is tied on 237 when D. Gough and D.G. Cork squared it for England as they completed a run from a bye ball

2005 New Zealand record the top score at the ground: 561 (H.J.H. Marshall 160, N.J. Astle 114, B.B. McCullum 99) against Sri Lanka

2007 West Indian C.H. Gayle scores record individual score on the ground, 197 out of 375

2008 In an excellent Third Test New Zealand score 431 chasing 553 in their second innings, T.G. Southee (77*) and C.S. Martin (5) putting on 84 for tenth wicket. Earlier a century for K.P. Pietersen (129) in the first innings; Sidebottom's ground best figures of 7–47 in New Zealand's first and centuries for A.J. Strauss (177) and I.R. Bell (110) had set up the run chase

2008 Fourth ODI of the series tied in a fantastic high-scoring game as New Zealand score a single off the last ball. Earlier J. How's 139 (116 balls, 3 sixes, 10 fours) almost secures victory

In recent times the Napier ground, home to the Central Districts team, has become more of a one-day international venue than a host ground for tests. The first test match held at McLean Park took place in 1979 as Pakistan played out a draw with New Zealand, Asif Iqbal scoring 104 in the visitors' first innings. Geoff Howarth responded with a century for the home team which Majid Khan matched in the Pakistan second innings.

The initial one-day contest of 1983 against Sri Lanka saw NZ comfortably brush aside Sri Lanka by 7 wickets in a low-scoring game. In 1990 two tests were played against India and one versus Sri Lanka, a feature of which was the bowling of Vaas who claimed match figures of 10 for 90. In December 2002 the visiting Indians were defeated in a one-dayer and in 2004, both Pakistan and South Africa came off second best in the shortened game.

When Sri Lanka arrived for test match action in 2005, a draw ensued after New Zealand's first innings of 561 received a response of 498 from the visitors; four centuries were scored during the game. Hamish Marshall and Nathan Astle did the honours for the home side, Atapattu and Jayawardene responding in kind.

RIGHT: McLean Park during the third ODI of the series against England, 20 February 2002. England won by 43 runs, P.D. Collingwood taking 4–38 from eight overs. *Tom Shaw/Getty Images 1095477*

WELLINGTON—WESTPAC AND BASIN RESERVE

WELLINGTON WESTPAC

Address: Wellington, New Zealand
Website: http://www.westpacstadium.co.nz/
Capacity: over 34,000
Opening Date: 2000

Memorable moments:

2000 First ODI results in an easy victory by 8 wickets for New Zealand over West Indies

2005 Australia win a high-scoring game by two runs with two run-outs in the last over: Australia 322–5 (A. Symonds 156 in 127 balls with 8 sixes and 12 fours), New Zealand 320

2006 First T20I victory for Sri Lanka by D/L method

WELLINGTON BASIN RESERVE

Address: Wellington, New Zealand
Website: http://www.cricketwellington.co.nz/
Capacity: 11,600
Opening Date: 1868

Memorable moments:

1930 First test, a draw against England, sees New Zealand score 440 in the first innings including a first-wicket partnership of 276 (C.S. Dempster 136, J.E. Mills 117), still the ground record

1975 First ODI is rained off after Bev Congdon's 101 took New Zealand to 227 against England

1991 New Zealand reply to Sri Lanka's 497 (P.A. da Silva 267) by scoring a ground-best total of 671–4 in the second (M.D. Crowe 299 and A.H. Jones 186; together they put on a ground record of 467 for the third wicket)

The beautiful Basin Reserve (known to locals as 'The Basin') is an old cricket ground in Wellington that has seen test, first-class and one-day cricket since its construction in 1868. On the National Heritage list and protected by act of parliament, it is probably the most beautiful cricket ground in New Zealand, perfectly placed in the middle of the city. The drawback of this is that it cannot be extended, and its limited capacity led to many ODIs and T20Is going to grounds outside Wellington. In an effort to combat this, Westpac Stadium—previously known as WestpacTrust Stadium, but called the 'Cake Tin' by locals—with a capacity of three times that of the Basin, provides a larger-capacity venue for One Day International cricket events.

To date (January 2009), 16 ODIs and a single T20I have been played at Westpac, New Zealand having won ten of the ODIs, including two close games in 2004 by 4 runs (against pakistan) and 5 runs (South Africa.

At the Basin New Zealand has fared well since losing seven of the first ten games played there. It won its first test at the ground, against the West Indies in 1969, some 39 years after the first test was played in Wellington. Unbeaten at the Basin between 1969 and 1994, New Zealand's record since 1969 is won 14, lost 8, drawn 15. Since 1994 it has been a result ground, with only three draws in the last 20 games.

RIGHT: The sun sets over Westpac Stadium during the first ODI of the Chappell-Hadlee Trophy series between New Zealand and Australia, 16 February 2007. Australia's meager 148 from 50 overs was achieved in 27 overs by L. Vincent (73*) and S.P. Fleming (70*) to give a 10-wicket margin of victory. *Phil Walter/Getty Images 73342281*

FAISALABAD—IQBAL STADIUM

IQBAL STADIUM

Address: Faisalabad, Pakistan
Capacity: 25,000
Opening Date: First-class cricket played since 1966

Memorable moments:

1978　First test match—against India—is drawn. Zaheer Abbas (176) and Javed Miandad (154*) put on 255 for the fourth wicket, a record until 1983

1982　Pakistan wins its first match at the stadium by an innings and three runs, scoring 501 (Zaheer Abbas 126 and Mansoor Akhtar 111)

1983　Pakistan scored 652 (Zaheer Abbas 168, Javed Miandad 126, Imran Khan 117, Saleem Malik 107) including a fourth-wicket partnership of 287

1984　Pakistan defeats New Zealand in the ground's first ODI by 5 runs

1985　Qasim Umar 206 and Javed Miandad 203* put on a record 397 for the third wicket against Sri Lanka

1986　Chasing 240 Abdul Qadir takes 9.3-1-16-6 and bowls out the West Indies for 53

1990　New Zealand's C. Pringle takes ground-best 7–52 in Pakistan's first innings and 4–100 in the second but is still on the losing side

1990　Waqar Younis has match figures of 12–130 as Pakistan beat New Zealand by 65 runs

1997　G. Kirsten (100*) bats through the first South African innings of 239; S.M. Pollock has figures of 11-1-37-5 as Pakistan are dismissed for 92 to lose by 53 runs

2003　Pakistan record the ground's best ODI score of 314–7 and beat New Zealand by 51 runs

2004　S.T. Jayasuriya scores ground's best, 253 against Sri Lanka

Named after Pakistan's national poet—Sir Allama Muhammad Iqbal—Iqbal Stadium is located in Faisalabad (previously called Lyallpur) the northwestern province of Punjab. In the past the Iqbal Stadium has had three other names: Lyallpur, National and City Stadium. A modern and well-equipped stadium—floodlights were installed in 2006—it has traditionally favoured batsmen, although two Pakistani bowlers found it helpful and stand out as the most successful in Faisalabad: Abdul Qadir, whose 42 wickets came at an average of 28.35 and Wasim Akram, whose 41 averaged 22.82 apiece.

While Pakistan have won six tests at Faisalabad (although none since 1996) and opponents five (the most successful being the West Indies with two), 12 of the 23 tests played here having ended in draws. The most successful batsman at the Iqbal is Pakistan legend Javed Miandad: in his 15 matches played on the ground he averaged 56.21 with five hundreds, two fifties and a top score of 203*.

Unfortunately, for many the ground is more famous for the confrontation between England captain Mike Gatting and umpire Shakoor Rana during the 1987–88 tour. The incident—which led to a day being lost during the match and a promising England position petering out to a draw—was one of the things that led to neutral umpires standing at test matches.

PREVIOUS PAGES: The Multan Cricket Stadium on day three of the First Test against England on 14 November 2005. Pakistan ended the third day on 125–2 in their second innings, still 19 runs behind. An English collapse on the final day, losing nine wickets for 111 runs, would see Pakistan become unlikely winners by 22 runs. *Julian Herbert/Getty Images 56155390*

RIGHT: The Iqbal Faisalabad Cricket Stadium on 22 November 2005, the third day of the Second Test against England. England ended the day on 391–7 still 71 runs behind Pakistan's first innings total. Another fifth-day collapse (England were 10–3 and 100–5) left the visitors happy to salvage a draw. *Stu Forster/Getty Images 56253944*

KARACHI—NATIONAL STADIUM

NATIONAL STADIUM

Address: Karachi, Pakistan
Capacity: 50,000
Opening Date: 1955

Memorable moments:

1955 First test match—against India—is drawn
1956 Australia bowled out for 80 in their first innings (Fazal Mahmood 6–34, Kan Mohammad 4–34) still a ground record. Pakistan win by 10 wickets
1980 First ODI played is a low-scoring cracker with West Indies winning by scoring four runs off the last ball chasing 128
1982 Imran Khan takes a ground best 8–60 in the second innings (adding to 3–19 in the first) and Pakistan beat India by an innings
1988 Javed Miandad scores 211 against Australia, a ground record. Pakistan win by an innings
1994 Pakistan beat Australia by one wicket chasing 315 thanks to a tenth wicket partnership of 57 by Inzamam-ul-Haq (58*) and Mushtaq Ahmed (20*)
1996 Quarter-final of the World Cup between South Africa and the West Indies sees South Africa fall 19 runs short chasing 264 (Lara scored 111)
1997 Aamir Sohail (160) and Ijaz Ahmed (151) put on a record 298 for the first wicket against the West Indies. Pakistan win by 10 wickets
2006 Pakistan score highest total on the ground, 599–7d (Faisal Iqbal 139) against India and win by 341 runs
2008 First T20I sees Pakistan beat Bangladesh by 102 runs after scoring 203 (Misbah-ul-Haq 87* from 53 balls; 14 sixes hit in the innings)

When built, Karachi's National Stadium became the city's fifth first-class ground and the second venue to stage test matches. After that first test against India in 1955 it took until 2000 before a Pakistan team would taste defeat in its former capital, a sequence of 34 games. The first one-day international in 1980 was lost when the West Indies scored the winning runs off the last available ball.

Although half of the games during the unbeaten test run were drawn, there were some sweet victories to be savoured—in particular the 1956 game in which Australia were dismissed for 80 in their first innings and defeated by nine wickets. The 1978 eight-wicket win over India engendered much rejoicing as Gavaskar had scored a century in both innings for the visitors, normally a platform for victory. This was countered by a Javed Miandad century complemented by a nine-wicket bowling haul from Sarfraz Nawaz. Thrilling victories over England in 1984 and Australia ten years later are still savoured and a series win over India, clinched at the stadium in early 2006, confirmed yet again what a fortress the National Stadium is.

Two unfortunate issues regarding this venue exist. There has been a marked reduction in attendances for test matches, one-dayers being much preferred, and, secondly, a perceived terrorist threat has meant certain touring sides have rejected requests to play there.

RIGHT: The Hong Kong (L) and Pakistan teams practice at the National Stadium on 22 June 2008 before the opening Group B match of the six-nation Asia Cup. Pakistan scored 288–9 and won by 155 runs. *Asif Hassan/AFP/Getty Images 81663406*

LEFT: The National Stadium on 5 October 2007 during day five of the First Test against South Africa. Five wickets for D.W. Steyn (5–65) ensured a comfortable win for the visitors. *Lee Warren/Gallo Images/Getty Images 77198648*

ABOVE: The 40-over ODI at Karachi on 26 March 1984 saw England win by six wickets thanks to Mike Gatting's all-round performance (3–32 and 38*). *Adrian Murrell/Getty Images 1242685*

LAHORE—GADDAFI STADIUM

GADDAFI STADIUM

Address: Lahore, Pakistan
Capacity: c50,000
Opening Date: 1959

Memorable moments:
1959 Australia win first test on the ground by seven wickets
1978 Pakistan win first ODI on the ground by 36 runs, bowling England out for 122
1982 Imran Khan had match figures of 14 for 116 in the innings victory over Sri Lanka
1987 Pakistan beat England by an innings and 87 thanks to Abdul Qadir's 9–56 in the first innings and 4–45 in the second
1989 Pakistan answer India's first-innings score of 509 (S.V. Manjrekar 218) with a massive ground-record 699–5 (Shoaib Mohammad, 203*, Javed Miandad 145, Aamer Malik 113)
1996 Hosted the final of the World Cup
2002 After Pakistan score 643 in the first innings (Inzamam-ul-Haq a record 329, Imran Nazir 127) New Zealand are bowled out for a ground-lowest 73 (Shoaib Akhtar 8.2-4-11-6) and 246, losing by an innings and 324
2006 After Pakistan raise 679–7d (Younis Khan 199, Mohammad Yousuf 173, Shahid Afridi 103, Kamran Akmal 102*) India respond with a ground record 410 for the first wicket (V. Sehwag 254 in 247 balls with a six and 47 fours; R. Dravid 128*)
2008 Sri Lanka hoist a ground-record 357–9 off 50 overs in an ODI against Bangladesh who lose by 131 runs

The Lahore Stadium, built in 1959, suffered from serious neglect for a number of years and in 1974 was renamed the Gaddafi Stadium. Just over twenty years later, due to the imminence of the 1996 Cricket World Cup, a decision to renovate the ground found a benefactor in the Libyan leader, Colonel Gaddafi, who came up with the necessary finance.

Architect Nayyar Ali Dadda went for a mixture of ancient and modern in his design, incorporating traditional red brick-work and Mughal-influenced arches into a thoroughly modern stadium. The ground is completely covered, using plastic seats in all areas and utilising the space under the stands for shops and offices. The installation of floodlights, an innovation for Pakistani venues, and contemporary media facilities added to the re-shaped ground's appeal.

Private boxes can be found in the large pavilion which overlooks a grassed area for players and officials. Around the ground are numerous enclosures named after various Pakistani cricketing heroes like Waqar Younis, Hanif Mohammad, Saeed Anwar and Khan Mohammad. The pavilion is flanked by two VIP enclosures carrying the names of Imran Khan and Fazal Mahmood. Despite its modernity, complaints are still made about the venue's lack of toilet facilities.

The huge crowd of over 60,000 which packed the ground for the 1996 World Cup Final is a rarity for Lahore as, mirroring the situation in Karachi, test matches can be played out in front of sparse crowds far outweighed by their one-day equivalents.

RIGHT: A view of the empty stands at Lahore on 11 March 2004 during a warm-up match between India and Pakistan 'A'. India and Pakistan kicked-off their cricket series, being played after a gap of fourteen years, with a test at Multan, won by India. Karachi hosted the Second Test—a victory by nine wickets for Pakistan. The series was decided in India's favour after the third and final test played at Rawalpindi Cricket Stadium. *Arko Datta/Reuters/Corbis DWF15-633024*

INSET: Pakistani legend Inzamam-ul-Haq waves to the crowd during a ceremony at the Gaddafi Stadium, 12 October 2007. Dismissed for three in his last test innings, he had fallen short of the record for most test runs for Pakistan. He finished with 8,830 runs in 120 tests, two short of Pakistan's record of 8,832 held by Javed Miandad. The match was drawn and South Africa went on to win the series 1–0. *Aamir Qureshi/AFP/Getty Images 77301454*

SOUTH AFRICA

BLOEMFONTEIN—OUTSURANCE OVAL

OUTSURANCE OVAL

Address: Bloemfontein, South Africa
Capacity: 19,000
Opening Date: 1989

Memorable moments:

1992 First ODI played at the ground sees South Africa beat India by 8 wickets chasing 208, A.C. Hudson scoring 108 to draw

1994 Australia (203) beat South Africa (202) by one run in the third ODI on the ground

1999 South Africa beat Zimbabwe by an innings and 13 runs in first test match on the ground

2000 J.H. Kallis scores a ground-best 160 out of 471 as New Zealand are beaten by an innings

2001 South Africa scores ground-best total of 563 (L. Klusener 108 and H.H. Gibbs 107). South Africa win by 9 wickets after S.M. Pollock takes 6–56 in the second innings

2001 Bowling hero Allan Donald took his 300th Test wicket when playing against New Zealand

2003 Hosted five games during the World Cup

2005 England (K.P. Pietersen 108) and South Africa (H.H. Gibbs 78) tie the second ODI of their series as A.J. Hall is stumped by G.O. Jones off Kabir Ali (3–56) from the last ball

2005 South Africa beat New Zealand by two wickets with three balls remaining, having chased 250

Recent years have seen the former Springbok Park and then Goodyear Park, now the Outsurance Oval, reduced to holding one-day internationals rather than test matches, the lack of spectator support being the main factor. For modern times it is unusual to find a major venue that still has vast expanses of grass for spectators to view from but this ground is one of them; an embankment shaded with trees runs along its eastern flank and there is a further stretch of greenery in front of the Centenary Stand on the opposite side.

To the south stands the pavilion and the scoreboard, which are divided by the Long Room bar; the north has another pavilion, a bank of seats plus the scoreboard. It is claimed that the ground has the best floodlights in world cricket. Local rugby side the Free State Cheetahs share the venue.

The Park only arrived on the test circuit in 1999, Zimbabwe being the hapless victims as South Africa romped to an innings win. The following year Jacques Kallis's 160 put SA on the road to a five-wicket victory over New Zealand. In 2001 India became victim number three in Bloemfontein, a nine-wicket defeat being inflicted upon them despite centuries from Sachin Tendulkar and Virender Sehwag. Lance Klusener and Herschelle Gibbs (with the bat) and Shaun Pollock (with the ball) took the honours for the home team.

In 2003 the ground hosted a number of matches in the World Cup, with Kenya, Zimbabwe, Holland and Namibia among the teams on view.

PREVIOUS PAGES: Kingsmead Stadium after the power had been switched off on 7 February 2007 during the second ODI between South Africa and Pakistan. Pakistan had scored 351–4 at the end of 50 overs (Mohammad Yousuf 101*, Younis Khan 93); South Africa could only manage 210. *Alexander Joe/AFP/Getty Images 73244443*

RIGHT: Goodyear Park during the World Cup Super Six ODI between Kenya and Zimbabwe on 12 March 2003. Kenya won by 7 wickets chasing 134. *Stu Forster/Getty Images 1858047*

CAPE TOWN—NEWLANDS

NEWLANDS

Address: Cape Town, South Africa
Capacity: 25,000
Opening Date: 1889

Memorable moments:

1889   First test match at the ground sees England winning by an innings and 202 runs. After England score 292 (R. Abel 120; W.H. Ashley 7–95) South Africa are dismissed for 47 (A.B. Tancred 26* batting through innings; J. Briggs 19.1-11-17-7) and 43 (Briggs 14.2-5-11-8) the second- and third- lowest scores on the ground

1899   South Africa lose by 210 runs after being dismissed for ground-lowest 35 (S. Haigh 11.4-6-11-6) in second innings

1923   South Africa (113 and 242) lose to England (183 and 173–9) by one wicket in spite of A.E. Hall's 7–63

1992   South Africa beat India by six wickets with three balls remaining in the first ODI on the ground

2001   South Africa raise a ground-best 354–3 (N.D. McKenzie 131*, G. Kirsten 124) in a 50 over ODI against Kenya

2003   South Africa hit ground-best 620–7d including a first wicket partnership of 368 (H.H. Gibbs 228, G.C. Smith 151). Pakistan lose by an innings

2003   Hosted four matches in the World Cup

2006   S.P. Fleming hits ground-best individual score of 262; match is drawn as South Africa respond with 512 (H.M. Amla 149, A.G. Prince 108*)

2007   Zimbabwe win first T20I on ground, beating Australia by five wickets with one ball remaining in the ICC World Twenty20

Situated at the foot of Table Mountain, Newlands, the home to Western Province has one of most idyllic settings in world cricket. It has hosted international cricket ever since its first test match in 1889, apart from a gap of twenty three years from 1970 when the country was excluded from the international arena. Recent changes to the ground are regretted by some, who still yearn for the old grassed embankments which have been replaced by pavilions.

South Africa's track record at Newlands was truly abysmal until they beat Australia in 1970: prior to that, they had only won one test, against England back in 1906. That very first test in 1889 had seen them bowled out for 47 and 43: the visitors' Johnny Briggs returned remarkable match figures of 15 wickets for 28 runs. Subsequently, all the other major international teams except Australia have come to grief at least once.

Herschelle Gibbs obviously has a liking for the ground; in 2003 he scored the second fastest double century of all time, sharing an opening partnership of 368 with Graeme Smith against Pakistan, and in 2004 was joined by Jacques Kallis in a third-wicket partnership of 251 versus the West Indies. Both Shaun Pollock and Allan Donald have taken over thirty wickets apiece in Cape Town at very little cost.

RIGHT: Newlands Cricket Ground on 15 September 2007 during the ICC Twenty20 World Championship match between South Africa and Bangladesh. South Africa won by seven wickets with seven balls remaining, scoring 145 thanks to M. Morkel's 41 off 29 balls and G.C. Smiths 41 which contained six sixes. *Tom Shaw/Getty Images 76773893*

BELOW: The opening match of the 2003 ICC Cricket World Cup was at Newlands between South Africa and the West Indies. The hosts scored the 145 they were set, winning by seven wickets with seven balls remaining. *Clive Mason/Getty Images 1796986*

ABOVE: The fourth ODI of their South African tour saw England at Newlands on 6 February 2005. The hosts' 291–5 (H.H. Gibbs 100) proved 108 runs too many for England. *Tom Shaw/Getty Images 52143762*

CENTURION—SUPERSPORT PARK

SUPERSPORT PARK

Address: Centurion, South Africa
Capacity: 20,000
Opening Date: 1986

Memorable moments:

1992   India win the first ODI on the ground by four wickets with five balls remaining

1995   First test on the ground is a rain-affected draw against England

2000   In a rain-affected match both sides forfeit an innings. England chase 249 to win by two wickets

2003   Five games in the World Cup took place in Centurion

2004   Herschelle Gibbs (192, ground best) and Graeme Smith (139) put on 301 for the first wicket in South Africa's ground-best first innings of 604–6d against West Indies. South Africa win by ten wickets

2005   M. Zondeki takes a ground-best 6–39 in the second innings (to add to his 3–66 in the first) as South Africa win by an innings and 62 runs

2008   A.G. Prince (162*) and M.V. Boucher (117) put on 271 for the sixth wicket in the innings win against Bangladesh

Despite being one of the world's younger test venues, the former Centurion Park has rapidly earned itself a reputation for excellence both on and off the pitch. Described by more than one test captain as having 'the best players' facilities in the world', the wicket has also come in for praise as its pace gives both fast bowler and batsman a sporting chance.

The ground's dominant structure is the imposing grandstand on the north side, offset against the other three sides which have grassy banks covered by seating and chalet-style corporate boxes. The general first-class facilities for the spectator have received positive comment from all who have watched cricket there.

Test cricket arrived in Centurion in November 1995 when England were the only side to bat in a badly rain-affected match. Two years later the elements were much kinder and Australia were beaten by eight wickets. In 1999 a struggling West Indies side came to the last test 4–0 down and failed to avoid the whitewash as they lost by 351 runs.

The lost 2000 game against England when a result was 'contrived' on the final day, became but a slightly nagging memory when the Second Test versus Sri Lanka in 2002 produced some excellent cricket in a topsy-turvy contest; South Africa ran out victors by three wickets.

The home side's record at SuperSport continued in 2005 with a resounding test win over Zimbabwe and a comfortable one-day triumph against New Zealand.

RIGHT: Centurion Park during the ODI against New Zealand, 25 October 2000. Another score over 300 for South Africa ensured victory by 115 runs. N. Boje scored 129 and Gary Kirsten 94 out of 324, and New Zealand could only manage 189 chasing the revised target of 300. Touchline *Photo/Getty Images 1710763*

LEFT: The fourth day of the Fifth Test against England at the Centurion Cricket Ground on 24 January 2005. South Africa declared leaving England a target of 185 in 40 overs on the final day. The visitors, at one time 20–3 in 15 overs, ground out a draw, ending on 73–4. *Clive Mason/Getty Images 52054835*

ABOVE: SuperSport Park during the First Test between South Africa and Pakistan in 2007. South Africa won here (by seven wickets) and at Cape Town (by five wickets), winning the series. Pakistan won the Second Test, played at St George's Park, Port Elizabeth. *Stu Forster/Getty Images 1807388*

DURBAN—SAHARA STADIUM KINGSMEAD

SAHARA STADIUM KINGSMEAD

Address: Kingsmead, Durban, South Africa
Capacity: 25,000
Opening Date: 1923

Memorable moments:

1923 First test match to be played was a draw between South Africa and England

1939 The unique 'Timeless Test' ends with England on 654–5 (W.J. Edrich 219, W.R. Hammond 140, P.A. Gibb 120) chasing 696 when England had to abandon to catch the boat home. A draw was declared

1948 England win by two wickets scoring 128–8. C.N. McCarthy's 6–43 almost wins it for South Africa

1992 First ODI on the ground saw South Africa beat India by 39 runs

1996 South Africa win by an innings after dismissing India for 100 (A.A. Donald 5–40) and 66 (ground record; Donald 11.1-4-14-4)

1999 Following on, South Africa score 572–7 (G. Kirsten ground best 275, M.V. Boucher 108) to save the match against England

2003 The World Cup semi-final between India (270, S.C. Ganguly 111*) and Kenya (179) sees India progress. they lose the final against Australia

2007 New Zealand beat Kenya by nine wickets in the first T20I on the ground

2008 South Africa hoist ground record total of 658 (J.H. Kallis 177, H.H. Gibbs 142, G. Kirsten 137) and beat the West Indies by an innings

In 1923 Kingsmead became the second venue in Durban to hold test matches when the third match in the series against England was drawn. England were the only visitors until 1935 when Australia claimed a nine-wicket victory.

The Third Test of 1959 was eventually won by Australia but only after two spectacular batting collapses, the visitors only managing 75 in their first innings and SA disastrously slumping to 99 all out in their second. In 1996, India surpassed both of these forgettable episodes when they were bowled out for 66.

At the other end of the scale South Africa's total of 622 for 9 declared set up an innings victory over Australia in 1970, Graeme Pollock and Barry Richards scoring 274 and 140 respectively. This was not the highest score Kingsmead has seen, for in 2004 the West Indies had to toil long in the field as SA made them pay with 658 for 9 declared. Runs were not exactly in short supply during the test in December 2004; Jacques Kallis helping himself to 162 and Trescothick, Strauss and Thorpe recording centuries in an England total of over 500.

The ground itself has a reputation as a venue famous for thunderstorms and hours lost through bad light. The positives come from the quality of the wicket and generally well-regarded spectator comforts. Kingsmead retains the grass embankments which are still a feature at many South African cricket stadiums.

RIGHT: Kingsmead on 25 March 2006 as South Africa's first innings continues under lights against Australia. Australia were earlier bowled out for 369 runs in their first innings. Bad light ended play early, with South Africa trailing by 229 runs with 8 wickets remaining in their first innings. Australia won the test series 3–0. *Jon Hrusa/epa/Corbis 42-16593756*

BELOW: Another view of the Sahara Stadium at Kingsmead on 7 February 2007 during the second ODI between South Africa and Pakistan—this time in daylight.
Gallo Images/Getty Images 73240205

ABOVE: Day two of the Third Test against the West Indies on 11 January 2008. South Africa won by an innings and 100 runs, their 556–4 (G.C. Smith 147, A.G. Prince 123*, A.B. de Villiers 103*) proving too much for the visitors. *Tertius Pickard/Gallo Images/Getty Images 78911054*

EAST LONDON—BUFFALO PARK

BUFFALO PARK

Address: East London, South Africa
Capacity: 15,000
Opening Date: 2002

Memorable moments:

1992   In the first ODI on the ground 2002 India beat South Africa by five wickets with 16 balls remaining

1993   Pakistan win an ODI by 9 runs as South Africa lose last seven wickets for 11 runs. Wasim Akram has figures of 6.1-0-16-5

2002   First test on the ground sees South Africa score 529 (G.C. Smith 200, G. Kirsten 150) and beat Bangladesh by an innings

2003   Three matches were held at the ground during the World Cup

2005   South Africa (311, G.C. Smith 115*) win a 50-over ODI by seven wickets defeating England (304, K.P. Pietersen 100*)

Nestling close to the Indian Ocean, Buffalo Park would figure in any contest for the most picturesque of grounds. As it is the smallest of all South African cricket venues, there is constant talk and anticipation of how development may take place. At the Buffalo Drive end of the ground the pavilion houses the press boxes and dressing rooms but it could be argued that the most impressive area is the enormous uncovered grass embankment to its left. Opposite the pavilion lies the main stand which runs out at another grass embankment which occasionally sports a temporary stand. There are two appropriately positioned scoreboards.

In the limited number of international matches East London has seen there have been, nonetheless, a number of significant performances.

Gary Kirsten scored 150 and Graeme Smith 200 in the inaugural test match against Bangladesh in 2002. Three years earlier in a one-day international, Shivnarine Chanderpaul and Carl Hooper shared a fourth-wicket partnership of 226 for the West Indies, in a match that Shaun Pollock took 6 for 35. In 1994, Waqar Younis took a hat-trick against New Zealand.

The most exciting match by a long way was the last one-dayer against England in 2005, eventually ending in a home win by 7 runs. Graeme Smith and Justin Kemp put on 117 for the fifth wicket and this proved the deciding factor, despite England's Kevin Pietersen hammering a 69-ball century (a limited-over record) for the visitors.

RIGHT: England playing a Border XI at Buffalo Park—the smallest ground in South Africa—on 6 February 2003. While it has been used for ODIs and a single test in 2002, it needs development before it becomes a regular international venue. *Tom Shaw/Getty Images 1764061*

INSET: On 17 December 1999 England played a four-day game against Eastern Province/Border XI at Buffalo Park. A beautiful arena, with a brilliant lighting system, it is a ground with a future. *Laurence Griffiths/Allsport 1204922*

JOHANNESBURG—THE WANDERERS

THE WANDERERS

Address: Corlett Drive, Illovo, Johannesburg
Capacity: 34,000
Opening Date: 1955

Memorable moments:

1956　England win first test at the Wanderers by 131 runs bowling South Africa out for ground's lowest 72 (T.E. Bailey 15.4-6-20-5) in their second innings

1957　Hugh Tayfield took a ground-best 9–113 in the second innings (4–79 in the first) to dismiss England for 214 and give victory to South Africa

1992　South Africa won first ODI at the ground by beating India by six wickets with nine balls remaining

1997　Australia score 628–8d including a fifth-wicket partnership of 385 (G.S. Blewett 214, S.R. Waugh 160) in an innings victory

2002　Australia score a ground-best 652–7d (A.C. Gilchrist 204*, D.R. Martyn 133, M.L. Hayden 122) and beat South Africa by 360 runs

2003　Hosted the World Cup Final when Australia beat India by 125 runs

2005　First T20I sees New Zealand beat South Africa by five wickets with 12 balls remaining

2006　Australia score 294–8 (D.R. Martyn 101) in the fourth innings to win a tight match by two wickets

2006　Australia 434 (R.T. Ponting 164) lose by one wicket with one ball remaining as South Africa chase down 438–9 (H.H. Gibbs 175, G.C. Smith 90)

2007　H.M. Amla (176*) and J.H. Kallis (186) put on 330 for the third wicket in the 358-run victory over New Zealand

In December 1956 the Wanderers became the third ground in South Africa to become a test venue. Since that country's return to the international stage in 1991, money has been made available to improve what is now the largest cricket venue in South Africa. An intimidating atmosphere has brought it the nickname of the Bullring.

At the southern end of the ground can be found the Unity Stand, completed in November 1992 and opened by the late Sir Colin Cowdrey.

Alongside sits the Taverners Pavilion; these structures are faced by the 1994 built Memorial Stand and the Centenary Pavilion. The Western Pavilion, refurbished in the mid-1990s and fronted by a grass bank, houses the dressing rooms. On the eastern side are further uncovered seats and a large replay screen, installed in 1996 when the lights were improved. In 2003, a fire that started in the kitchens gutted the clubhouse, destroying many irreplaceable artefacts and memorabilia.

The Wanderers has seen mixed results for the home side in its time, three substantial victories over Australia between 1966 and 1970 having been overshadowed by hefty innings defeats at the Aussies' hands in 1997 and 2002. In the second of these Adam Gilchrist hit what was the fastest double century in test history (204* in 213 balls and 293 minutes with eight sixes and 19 fours). Another innings from a visiting player worthy of note was the eleven-hour marathon from Mike Atherton, when his 185 not out salvaged a draw for England in 1995. But nothing can compare with the fifth ODI of the Australian tour in 1996 when South Africa overhauled 434–4 to win by one wicket with one ball remaining—a truly remarkable match.

RIGHT: This aerial view of the Wanderers shows the ground before the redevelopment had been finished. Looking over the top of the Centenary Pavilion and the Memorial Stand—the Golf Course End—towards, at the top of the picture, the imposing Unity Stand; the new floodlights (which were put in during 1996) and the Kent Park Taverners Pavilion at the Corlett Drive End which was pulled down and rebuilt before the 2003 World Cup, have still to go in. *Paul Velasco; Gallo Images/Corbis AB005334*

LEFT: On 13 September 2007 the shellshocked West Indies played Bangladesh during the ICC World Twenty20 Championship. They lost again, their target of 164 achieved by Bangladesh in 18 overs, captain Mohammad Ashraful scoring 61 from 27 balls. This picture shows the Unity Stand that was officially opened on 26 November 1992 by Sir Colin Cowdrey, before the first test match at the ground in 22 years took place. To the left of the Unity Stand is the rebuilt Kent Park Taverners Pavilion that took ground capacity to 34,000. *Julian Herbert/Getty Images 76712663*

PORT ELIZABETH—ST GEORGE'S PARK

ST GEORGE'S PARK

Address: Port Elizabeth, South Africa
Capacity: 19,000
Opening Date: 1888

Memorable moments:

1889   England win the first test at the ground by eight wickets

1896   England's George Lohmann returns match figures of 15.4-6-38-7 and 9.4-5-7-8 as South Africa are dismissed for 93 and 30 to lose by an innings

1950   Australia score a ground-best 549 (A.L. Hassett 167, A.R. Morris 157, R.N. Harvey 116) winning by an innings

1970   South Africa beat Australia by 323 runs scoring 470–8d in their second innings (B.A. Richards 126, B.L. Irvine 102) and Mike Proctor taking 6–73 to dismiss Australia for 246

1992   South Africa beat India in the first ODI on the ground winning by six wickets with 20 balls remaining

1997   Australia chase 270 in the fourth innings and win by two wickets (M.E. Waugh 116)

2001   H.H. Gibbs scores a ground-best 196 against India

2002   Saleem Elahi (135) and Abdul Razzaq (112) put on 257 for the second wicket in the second ODI, leading to a win by 182 runs

2003   Hosted five games during the World Cup including the Australia v Sri Lanka semi-final

2007   West Indies won the first T20I on the ground by five wickets

St George's Park sits very much at the centre of South African sporting history, having staged both the country's first rugby international in 1891, the first test to be held outside Australia or England in 1888 and, less gloriously, the final test before a ban from sporting competition in 1970.

It took until 1954, with a five-wicket victory over New Zealand, for the Proteas to record their first win in Port Elizabeth, although this was only the sixth test to be held there. In a fluctuating contest played in 1949, SA come close to surprising the English tourists but in a last-ditch effort to level the five-match series, they eventually went down by 3 wickets.

That last test before isolation did bring some satisfaction as the hosts completed a 4-0 series win over Australia, the influential players being Barry Richards, Lee Irvine and Mike Proctor.

Typically, St George's mixes covered areas with those open to the elements and reflects the redevelopment that took place in 1993 when a new stand was built at the northern Duckpond end. At the southern end stands the Centenary Pavilion, the Media Centre and hospitality chalets. There are more of these chalets on the west side, standing cheek by jowl with the Frielinghaus Stand and the main scoreboard.

It has been suggested that this Port Elizabeth location is more intimate in nature than larger test grounds, although some of that intimacy may disappear when the famed local winds are blowing.

RIGHT: St George's Park on 9 December 1999—the first day of the drawn second test between England (373, M.A. Atherton 108, and 153–6 set 302) and South Africa (450, L. Klusener 174, and 224–4d). *Stu Forster/Allsport/Getty Images 1211961*

GALLE INTERNATIONAL STADIUM

GALLE INTERNATIONAL STADIUM

Address: Galle, Sri Lanka
Capacity: 10,000
Opening Date: 1996

Memorable moments:

1998   Sri Lanka win the first test match on the ground against New Zealand by an innings. D.P.M.D. Jayawardene scores 167

1998   The first ODI due to be played against India is abandoned without a ball being bowled

2000   Pakistan scored the ground's top total of 600–8d (Saeed Anwar 123, Younis Khan 116, Inzamam-ul-Haq 112, Wasim Akram 100) and beat Sri Lanka by an innings and 163 runs

2001   Host for the First Test against England. Sri Lanka win by an innings and 28 runs, scoring 470–5d (M.S. Atapattu 201*, P.A. da Silva 106 put on 230 for the third wicket)

2002   Zimbabwe are dismissed for a ground's lowest 79 in their second innings and lose by 315 runs

2003   M. Muralitharan takes 7–46 in England's first innings and 4–47 in their second but they hold out for the draw on 210–9

2004   D.P.M.D. Jayawardene scores 237, the ground's highest individual score

2004   Australia score 512–8d (M.L. Hayden 130, D.S. Lehmann 129, D.R. Martyn 110) in their second innings and S.K. Warne takes 5–43 in Sri Lanka's second innings and Australia win by 197 runs

2007   Sri Lanka score 499–8d (D.P.M.D. Jayawardene 213*) and England are dismissed for 81 in their first innings; but England bat through the final day to draw

ntil the tsunami struck Galle in December 2004, the ground was viewed as one of the most beautiful venues on the test circuit, with the Indian Ocean on either side and the 16th-century Dutch fort just outside the ground a unique landmark. First-class cricket came to Galle, once grandly named the Esplanade, in 1984 and international cricket in 1998.

The ground had all the usual facilities one expects from a modern venue: sadly, the pavilion containing the dressing rooms and administration offices, the various VIP sections and the scoreboard that stood on the grass embankment known as 'The Hill' are no more. Such luminaries as Shane Warne and Ian Botham have been involved in encouraging the continuation of cricket in the area and the rebuilding of the stadium.

Sri Lanka have only lost two tests at this ground, which has seen Muralitharan take over 80 wickets; he opened his account against New Zealand in that first winning test of 1998 and has been a thorn in the side of visiting teams ever since. A draw against Australia in 1999 preceded a defeat a year later at the hands of Pakistan, who won by an innings and 163 runs after scoring 600 for 8 declared – a total including four centuries.

That same year the last one-day international seen at Galle to date took place in the Singer Triangular Series, the result a 37-run win for Sri Lanka over South Africa. South Africa, England, India and West Indies all suffered crushing defeats at the hands of the Tigers during 2000 and 2001.

ABOVE: Taken on 5 January 2005, former Sri Lankan cricketer Jayananda Warnaweera sits on debris strewn across the Galle pitch after the Asian tsunami. An international appeal ensured that the ground was ready for England's arrival in 2007. England were lucky to draw the match after Sri Lanka reached 499 (captain D.P.M.D. Jayawardene scoring 213), being dismissed for 81 and having to follow on. In the end rain helped them bat through two days to draw the match. *Jimin Lai/AFP/Getty Images 74969989*

BELOW: Galle stadium during the first day of the First Test between Sri Lanka (331 and 226) and England (235 and 210–9 chasing 323) on 2 December 2003. One of the world's most picturesque cricket venues, it is overlooked by a centuries-old Dutch Fort, and a clocktower built in 1881. *Stu Forster/Getty Images 2775424*

KANDY—ASGIRIYA STADIUM

ASGIRIYA STADIUM

Address: Kandy, Sri Lanka
Capacity: 15,000
Opening Date: 1983 (when redeveloped for test cricket)

Memorable moments:

1983　Became Sri Lanka's second Test venue when Australia visited. Sri Lanka lose by an innings and 38 after Australia score 514–4d (D.W. Hookes 143*, K.C. Wessels 141)

1994　Pakistan beat Sri Lanka by an innings, dismissing the home side for the ground's lowest test total of 71 in its first innings (Wasim Akram 4–32, Waqar Younis 6–34)

1996　Sri Lanka beat Kenya in a World Cup ODI, scoring ground record total of 398–5, P.A. da Silva scoring 145)

1998　Sri Lanka's first Asgiriya test win, Marvan Atapattu hitting 223 in Sri Lanka's first innings; M. Muralitharan taking 5–23 and 7–94 in Zimbabwe's innings

1998　First ODI on the ground: Pakistan win by eight wickets with nine balls remaining .

2000　M.S Atapattu (207*) and S.T. Jayasuriya (188) put on 335 for the first wicket against Pakistan, a record for any wicket for Sri Lanka

2002　M. Muralitharan records ground-best test match figures of 66.4-26-115-13 as Sri Lanka beat Zimbabwe by an innings

2007　K.C. Sangakkara (222*) D.P.M.D. Jayawardene (165) put on a ground test record 311 for the third wicket; M. Muralitharan takes 6–28 and 6–54 as Bangladesh lose by an innings

The Asgiriya Stadium is located within the playing fields of Trinity College, home of Kandy Cricket Club; the ground was created by carving a great chunk out of a suitable hill. The general consensus is that there are few prettier sporting venues in the world, cradled amongst the hills and lush vegetation and overlooked by a large image of the Buddha. Inside, there are two pavilions, the Old Trinity Clubhouse, a grandstand and popular uncovered areas. The catering facilities have come in for positive comments from more than one quarter.

Test cricket came to Kandy in 1983 when Australia trounced the home team by an innings and 38 runs; Sri Lanka also lost their first one-day international at the location when Pakistan romped home by 8 wickets.

The wait for a test victory lasted until 1998; the account was opened against Zimbabwe but the six-wicket triumph over Australia some twenty months later really made the cricket world sit up and notice.

Subsequently, results have been patchy, including a seven-run defeat to South Africa, an annihilation of Zimbabwe, a win over India and a twenty-seven run defeat to Australia.

The test of 2005 against the West Indies produced a second successive win against the tourists at the Asgiriya. Vaas claimed 6 wickets in the visitors' first innings, Sangakkara hitting 157 not out for the home side in their second and that most prolific of wicket takers, Muttiah Muralitharan, returning a match total of 10 for 83.

RIGHT: Day one of the First Test between Sri Lanka (188, K.C. Sangakkara 92, and 442–8d K.C. Sangakkara 152) and England (281 and 261 chasing 350) at the Asgiriya Stadium on 1 December 2007. The home ground of Trinity College, it is a beautiful venue high in Sri Lanka's hill country.
Stu Forster/Getty Images 78200603

WEST INDIES

LEFT: The Third Test of England's 2004 tour was played at Bridgetown. England (226, G.P. Thorpe 119*, and 93–2) beat the West Indies (224 and 94) by eight wickets. Since then the ground has been completely redeveloped. *Bob Thomas/Getty Images 78987974*

BRIDGETOWN—KENSINGTON OVAL

KENSINGTON OVAL

Address: Bridgetown, Barbados, West Indies
Capacity: 11,000 boosted to 27,000 for World Cup Final
Opening Date: 1871

Memorable moments:

1930 First test match is a draw against England. G.A. Headley scores 176 in West Indies' second innings

1955 Australia posts highest test total on the ground—668 (K.R. Miller 137, R.R. Lindwall 118, R.G. Archer 98). West Indies reply with 510, D.S. Atkinson (219) and C.C. Depeiaza (122) putting on 347 for the seventh wicket

1958 Pakistan's Hanif Mohammed played the longest innings in est history, spending 16 hours and 10 minutes at the wicket, accumulating 337 runs to save the match as Pakistan follow on

1985 First ODI on the ground sees West Indies beat New Zealand by 112 runs

1960 G.S. Sobers (226) and F.M.M. Worrell (197*) put on 399 for the fourth wicket against England

1962 Lance Gibbs takes 8–38 in India's second innings and West Indies win by an innings

1965 W.M. Lawry (210) and R.B. Simpson (201) put on 382 for the first wicket; in reply S.M. Nurse (201) and R.B. Kanhai put on 200 for the third wicket and the match is drawn

1985 West Indies beat New Zealand by 10 wickets. Malcolm Marshall has ground best match figures of 40.3-9-120-11

2007 Hosted the final of the World Cup: Australia beat Sri Lanka

2008 First T20I sees Australia defeated by 11 runs

The Kensington Oval underwent a major redevelopment programme in preparation for the 2007 World Cup, hence such structures as the Garfield Sobers Players' Pavilion, the Hall and Griffith Stand and the Kensington Stand were unrecognisable or no longer in existence when the new Oval was unveiled. At a cost of some US$45 million, the ground became an all-seater venue with an increased capacity of 27,000 for the World Cup final thanks to two temporary stands. Soon after demolition commenced in mid-2005, there were reports of the work falling behind schedule but the 2007 World Cup passed off without a hitch—except that the final was played out between Australia and Sri Lanka and the West Indies went out at an earlier stage.

Home to the Pickwick Cricket Club since 1882, the Oval featured international cricket as far back as 1895, with Test cricket arriving in 1930. The West Indies and England played out a draw, the great George Headley scoring a century for the home side on his debut.

Hanif's marathon innings apart, the Oval has been the stage for some spectacular scoring from individuals, including the 1960 runfest for Garry Sobers and Frank Worrell who racked up 226 and 197 not out respectively in a draw against England. Australians Bobby Simpson and Bill Lawry both scored double centuries in 1965 and West Indian Lawrence Rowe went one better, with a triple, nine years later.

Between 1948 and 1994 the ground was a West Indian fortress. Broken by England's 208-run win in 1994, New zealand, Australia and South Africa have also had victories at the Kensington Oval since.

RIGHT: The new Garfield Sobers Pavilion (L) and new Worrell, Weekes and Walcott Stand (R) seen while Ireland plays Australia during the ICC World Cup on 13 April 2007. Some people yearn for the intimacy of the old ground, where West Indies won 12 straight matches (1978–93) and went unbeaten from 1948 to 1994. *Adrian Dennis/AFP/Getty Images) 73875752*

TOTAL	17
WICKETS	0
OVERS	2.3
TARGET	92
GILCHRIST	5
HUSSEY	5
FALL OF WICKET	
OVERS REMAIN	48
RUNS TO WIN	75
RATE ACHIEVED	6.8
RATE REQUIRED	1.6
D/L PAR SCORE	
F/R BLOCK	BLK 1

GEORGETOWN—BOURDA

BOURDA

Address: Georgetown, Guyana, West Indies
Capacity: 22,000
Opening Date: 1884

Memorable moments:

1884   Georgetown Cricket Club played their first game at the ground

1930   West Indies beat England in the first test at the ground

1955   I.W.G. Johnson takes ground best 7–44 in West Indies second innings and Australia win by eight wickets

1968   In the drawn test against England Gary Sobers scored 152 and 95 not out, and took 6 match wickets

1972   G.M. Turner (259) and T.W. Jarvis (182) put on a ground record 387 for New Zealand's first wicket

1988   West Indies beat Pakistan in the first ODI at the ground

1988   Imran Khan takes ground-best match figures of 37.2-2-121-11 as Pakistan win by nine wickets

1993   West Indies and Pakistan tie ODI on 244

1991   West Indies score a ground-highest 569 (R.B. Richardson 182 and D.L. Haynes 111 put on 297 for the second wicket) beating Australia by 10 wickets

1999   West Indies and Australia tie rain-restricted ODI on 173

2002   C.L. Hooper (233) and S.Chanderpaul (140) put on 293 for the fifth wicket against India

2207   Bourda is replaced by the National Stadium in Providence as the Guyanan international arena

The Bourda ground is one of only two test venues in the world to sit below sea level and is accordingly protected by a moat. This location has been described as having an 'antique feel' and, affectionately by cricket-writer Mike Selvey, 'slightly scruffy'.

Many of the structures within its boundaries are steeped in history; the Ladies' Pavilion dates from 1912, the Members' Pavilion is constructed of wood and the scoreboard is as old as the ground. The Rohan Kanhai Stand from a much later date carries three tiers, looks rather splendid and contains a number of corporate boxes. The popular uncovered Mound area is famous for its music, beer-drinking and atmosphere.

The region is notorious for inclement weather and, over the decades, the Bourda has seen more than its fair share of draws. The easy pace of the pitch has not exactly assisted bowlers, either, as they have striven to acquire that elusive victory.

The Bourda's reputation for volatility which has hopefully been left behind was established in the 1970s. Two disputed decisions against West Indian batsman prompted unpleasant pitch invasions, while a Kerry Packer World Series game's abandonment caused a riot that reportedly led to players sheltering in the dressing rooms for protection.

Perhaps it is better to dwell on the first test match played in 1930 against England when George Headley scored a century in both innings as WI won by 289 runs, or the double centuries for both Hinds and Chanderpaul in the rain-affected 2005 contest versus South Africa.

RIGHT: Ground staff try to remove the water after heavy rain left the pitch looking like this on 16 April 2004. One of the oldest grounds in the Caribbean, Bourda is below sea level and this—and inclement weather—mean that this happens quite often. Note the lovely old wooden pavilion and stands. *Clive Rose/Getty Images 3415990*

LEFT: A Guyanan military helicopter is deployed to help dry the cricket pitch at Bourda. Play between England and the West Indies for the first ODI of the tour on 18 April 2004 was delayed by heavy rain. The match was restricted to 30 overs and saw England win by two wickets with three balls remaining, in spite of C.H. Gayle's 5.3-0-20-3.
Toby Melville/Reuters/ Corbis DWF15-679477

ABOVE: Guyana's new international stadium, purpose-built for the 2007 World Cup, is in Providence, about five miles south of Georgetown. It has an overall capacity of around 15,000 with three stands and a grass mound that can accommodate 4,000 people. To date it has only hosted a handful of ODIs and a solitary test match—the First Test against Sri Lanka on 23 March 2008. After Mahela Jayawardene had posted his 22nd test hundred (136), B.S.M. Warnapura scored 120 to help the visitors reach 476–8d in their first innings. The home team were all out for 280 and the visitors' second innings of 240 left the West Indies chasing a massive 437. They made a creditable 315. Here the pitch remains covered as it rains on and off prior to the start of the World Cup Super Eights match between Sri Lanka and South Africa on 28 March 2007. *Prakash Singh/AFP/Getty Images 73730568*

KINGSTON—SABINA PARK

SABINA PARK

Address: Kingston, Jamaica, West Indies
Capacity: 20,000
Opening Date: 1880

Memorable moments:

1930 First test match played on the ground is time-less. England score ground-record 849 (A. Sandham 325, ground record until 1958); draw agreed with West Indies 408–5 (G.A. Headley 223)

1958 Gary Sobers recorded the highest ever individual Test score of 365* against Pakistan. This stood until 1994 when Brian Lara surpassed it. West Indies post 790–3d and with C.C. Hunte (260) Sobers puts on 446 for the second wicket. West Indies win by an innings

1985 First ODI on ground sees West Indies beat Australia by nine wickets (Haynes 104*)

1990 West Indies beat England in ODI from last ball (R.B. Richardson 108*)

1999 B.C. Lara (213) and J.C. Adams (94) put on 322 for fifth wicket against Australia

2004 England dismiss West Indies for ground's lowest test score of 47 (S.J. Harmison 12.3-8-12-7—ground's best test figures) and win by 10 wickets

2006 West Indies win ODI against India in the last over by one run when Yuvraj Singh (93) is bowled by Bravo

2007 Imran Nazir scores ground-highest ODI score of 160 in World Cup match against Zimbabwe

2007 Sri Lanka beat New Zealand in World Cup ODI semi-finals

Sabina Park may be situated in an area populated by housing and offices but few cricket grounds can boast a vista quite as stunning as the Blue Mountains which can be seen from the location—but no longer from the square as it is blocked by the new North Stand.

Like all the other major Cribbean grounds, Sabina Park underwent a major renovation ahead of the 2007 World Cup—although the process was not straightforward and many locals felt that it removed the character of the ground. Such is the way of progress: the ground may not appear as it did, but the facilities are much improved as the photographs here attest. The capacity was raised from 15,000.

The concern over the pace of the wicket has led to it being relaid in recent times, for in the past Sabina Park always had a reputation as a fast track. This problem has not necessarily been a barrier to achieving positive results at the ground, but the ignominy of the 1998 test against England being abandoned because the pitch was declared dangerous suggested problems of a different kind.

The Kingston arena is no stranger to spectacular high scoring. England accumulated 849 runs in the first test played there in 1930, top scorer being Andy Sandham with 325.

The Sobers knock was, of course, quite special, but the famous three Ws of West Indian cricket turned in a wonderful display against India in 1953. Everton Weekes and Clive Walcott both scored centuries in the first innings but were topped by Frank Worrell's double.

Two years later the Australian batsman ran amok. Five players passed the hundred mark as the West Indies slumped to an innings defeat.

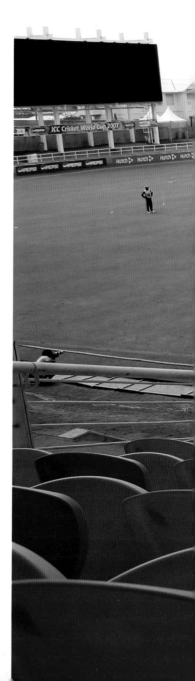

RIGHT: The Pakistan team plays football during the ICC Cricket World Cup on 20 March 2007. The next day Pakistan beat Zimbabwe by 93 runs (D/L method) in a rain-affected game. The visible stand is the George Headley stand that seats 6,000. At left the new scoreboard. *Paul Gilham/Getty Images) 73641358*

LEFT: Brett Lee of Australia bowls during day five of the First Test on 26 May 2008. Australia won after the West Indies, chasing 287, were all out for 191. Lee took 2–82; S.R. Clark 5–32. The photograph also shows off the old Members' Pavilion and its new, canopied roof. *Harry How/Getty Images 81239052*

RIGHT: Stuart Clark of Australia bowls during day three of the First Test on 24 May 2008. The hosts' first innings reached 312 (S. Chanderpaul 118) and at close Australia were only 17–4 (136 ahead). The next day, however, Symonds' 79 allowed them to reach 167 and, ultimately, victory. *Harry How/Getty Images 81224433*

QUEEN'S PARK OVAL

Address: Port of Spain, Trinidad, West Indies
Capacity: 25,000
Opening Date: 1896

Memorable moments:

1930 England win the first test on the ground by 167 runs thanks to fourth-wicket second-innings partnership of 237 by E.H. Hendren (205* and L.E.G. Ames 105) and 7–70 by Bill Voce

1954 West Indies 681–8d against England is ground's highest test total (E.D. Weekes 206, F.M.M. Worrell 167, C.L. Walcott 124 including ground's best partnership of 338 for the third wicket

1962 Two ground-best test partnerships in West Indies' seven-wicket win: 93 for the ninth by P.R. Umrigar (172*), R.G. Nadkarni (23); 98* for tenth by F.M.M. Worrell (73*), W.W. Hall (50*)

1971 J.M. Noriega takes 9–95 in India's first innings but West Indies still lose by seven wickets

1971 S.M. Gavaskar 220 is ground's highest test score

1983 First ODI on ground sees West Indies (D.L. Haynes 97) beat India by 52 runs

1974 Tony Greig has match figures of 13–156— ground's test best until 2005—and G. Boycott scores 99 and 112 as England win by 26 runs

2005 M. Ntini takes 13–132 in South Africa's eight-wicket win

2007 V. Sehwag (114) and S.C. Ganguly (89) put on ground's highest ODI partnership of 202 out of 413 scored against Bermuda during the World Cup. India win by 257 runs

2008 S. Chanderpaul (62*) leads West Indies to a final ball victory by one wicket against Sri Lanka

The Queen's Park Oval is currently the largest cricket ground in the Caribbean and reportedly the most profitable. For many a year the original pavilion built in 1896 stood at the heart of the ground and was replaced in 1952. The reworking of the ground prior to the 2007 World Cup included a new pavilion. The pavilion is situated at the southern end opposite the Media Centre end. On the off side three stands named after West Indian cricketing stalwarts are to be found, the trio being Learie Constantine, Jeff Stollmeyer and Errol Dos Santos. Before being renamed, the Constantine had carried the unprepossessing soubriquet of the 'Concrete Stand', but has remained a hotbed of passionate local support.

For decades the state of the pitch had caused some concern. In the early days turf was used, to be replaced by matting placed on concrete which became the norm at the Oval for some forty years before the eventual return to turf in 1954. With the 2007 World Cup coming to the West Indies, the pitch received much attention in 2006.

This is the ground much loved by India's Sunil Gavaskar who scored four centuries in five tests, where Patsy Hendren ensured an England victory in 1930 with 205 not out and the scene of Malcolm Marshall's best match return of 11 for 89. Curtly Ambrose also had an amazing record at the Oval; in 12 matches, he took 66 wickets at a cost of only 13.29 apiece.

ABOVE: Was there ever a greater fast bowling combination than this 1981 lineup? From L to R: Andy Roberts (202 test wickets at 25.61), Michael Holding (249 at 23.68), Colin Croft (125 at 23.30) and Joel Garner (259 at 20.97). *Adrian Murrell/Allsport 1270768*

BELOW: The pitch is covered due to heavy rain during the ICC Cricket World Cup 2007 Group B match between Bangladesh and Bermuda on 25 March 2007. In the end a 21-over match was played, Bangladesh winning by seven wickets. This view looks directly at the upgraded Gerry Gomez Media Centre which is flanked by the Learie Constantine and Cyril L. Duprey stands. Gomez was a famous West Indian captain and administrator; Duprey, the MD of a local insurance company; and Lord Learie Constantine was one of the great figures of cricket. *Clive Rose/Getty Images 73696751*

ST JOHN'S—ANTIGUA RECREATION GROUND

ANTIGUA RECREATION GROUND

Address: St John's, Antigua, West Indies
Capacity: 12,000
Opening Date: c1880

Memorable moments:

1978 First ODI on the ground is a West Indies win by 44 runs with ground's highest team (313–9) and individual (D.L. Haynes 148) scores

1981 First test match—between West Indies and England—is a draw

1984 Ground's best test opening third wicket partnership of 308 (I.V.A. Richards 178, R.B. Richardson 154) leads to an innings victory against Australia

1990 Ground's best test opening partnership of 298 (D.L. Haynes 167, C.G. Greenidge 149) leads to an innings victory against England

1994 B.C. Lara scores 375 out of 593–5d against England who also score 593 (R.A. Smith 175, M.A. Atherton 135)

2003 J.J.C. Lawson takes ground's test best 7–78 against Australia; West Indies score 418–7 (R.R. Sarwan 105, S. Chanderpaul 104) to win

2004 Against England West Indies score ground's highest score (751–5d) including sixth wicket partnership of 282* between B.C. Lara, who scores test cricket's highest individual score of 400* (four sixes and 43 fours), and R.D. Jacobs (107*)

2005 West Indies reply to South Africa's 588–6d (J.H. Kallis 147, A.G. Prince 131, G.C. Smith 126, A.B. de Villiers 114) with 747 (C.H. Gayle 317, R.R. Sarwan 127, S. Chanderpaul 127, D.J. Bravo 107) including ground's best second wicket test partnership of 331 between Gayle and Sarwan

The pitch is a notorious 'flat bed' which is always likely to produce batting records, and Brian Lara has twice been grateful for its benign nature. In 1994 he overtook Gary Sobers' long-standing individual test record when he scored 375 in a drawn match with England, only to better this figure ten years later against the same opponents with 400 not out. This left him with an average of over 90 in 12 matches in Antigua.

In 2003, WI scored over 400 in their second innings to achieve an unlikely win over Australia, Sarwan and Chanderpaul centuries paving the way.

The 2005 game against South Africa may have looked to be going the visitors' way as they piled up a total of 588 that included four centuries, only to be rebuffed by a reply of 747, three centurions being outscored by Gayle who made a triple century. Not surprisingly, the game petered out into a draw.

The closest game to be played was not high-scoring at all, for in 2000 the Pakistanis were beaten by one wicket, with neither side reaching 300 in any innings.

One of the most fascinating facts about the Recreation Ground involves the ground staff, who, for a period, were supplied by the local prison whose warden was Malcolm Richards, the father of local hero Viv.

A ground full of character—and characters: such as Gravy who disported himself on the double-deck stand—the Recreation Ground has always been a colourful venue much loved by local and tourist alike.

RIGHT: Black clouds hover over the field as England's cricketers go through a practice session at the Recreation Ground in St John's, 6 April 2007. It was not chosen for use as a World Cup venue, the Antiguan games being played at the Sir Vivian Richards Stadium built specially for the event (see page 183). *Jewel Samad/AFP/Getty Images 73826596*

ABOVE: Brian Lara of the West Indies runs the single to take his score past the previous world record, that of Matthew Hayden on 380, during day three of the Fourth Test between the West Indies and England at the Recreation Ground on 12 April 2004. He would go on to score 400*. *Tom Shaw/Getty Images 3342073*

RIGHT: The Sir Vivian Richards Stadium holds 10,000 people, but temporary seating doubled this for the World Cup. This view shows the North Stand during the Super Eights match between Australia and England at on 8 April 2007. The ground's sixth ODI of the cup, Australia won by seven wickets *Hamish Blair/Getty Images 73841557*

BELOW: The Arnos Vale Sports Complex in Kingstown, Saint Vincent and the Grenadines has to be one of the most dramatically sited venues in the world. It was used during the World Cup for warming up—here a match between Australia and Zimbabwe on 6 March 2007. *Tom Shaw/Getty Images 73510049*

RIGHT: Warner Park in Basseterre, St Kitts, was the first of the new grounds erected for use during the World Cup. It was funded by Taiwan and had a capacity of 10,000 by using temporary stands. Here a Group A match takes place between Australia and South Africa on 24 March 2007. *Shaun Botterill/Getty Images 73690322*

RIGHT: A dramatic view of the Stanford Cricket Ground, Coolidge, Antigua, during the Stanford Twenty20 Super Series match between Stanford Super Stars and Middlesex. Previously known as the Airport Cricket Ground, Stanford's money-based approach to the game did not win international plaudits. The Stanford Super Stars beat England on 1 November 2008 to win the tournament—and the huge prize money. Stanford's ground is a first-class facility, with an excellent grandstand and ground capacity of 5,000. *Tom Shaw/Getty Images 83498641*

DHAKA—BANGABANDHU AND SBNC STADIUMS

BANGABANDHU AND SBNC STADIUMS

Address: Dhaka, Bangladesh
Capacity: 36,000 (Bangabandhu); 47,000 (SBNC)
Opening Date: 1955 (Bangabandhu); 2006 (SBNC)

Memorable Moments (SBNC):
2006   First ODI win by eight wickets against Zimbabwe
2007   First test is a loss by an innings. India score 610–3d (W. Jaffer 138*, K.D. Karthik 129, R. Dravid 129, S.R. Tendulkar 122*)
2008   D.P.M.D. Jayawardene's 166 is ground's best individual test score
2008   Shahadat Hossain's 6–27 against South Africa is ground's best

Formerly known as both the Dacca Stadium and the National Stadium, the Bangabandhu holds a unique place in cricket history as the only ground to have held inaugural test matches for two separate countries—Pakistan and Bangladesh. Pakistan's tenure lasted until 1969, two years before the independent state of Bangladesh came into existence.

This is a large ground with a modern pavilion containing hospitality facilities, a members' area and changing rooms. Its three tiers sit above the neighbouring stands, which only rise to two. Some of the last development work carried out at the venue took place in 1998 with the installation of floodlights and an electronic scoreboard.

In March 2005 the ground was taken over for the exclusive use of the national football team. Even though noises were com-

ing from the cricketing authorities some months later regarding forthcoming match plans, the erection of a cricket-only venue—the SBNC Stadium—rather indicates that bat and ball may have made a permanent exit.

Bangladesh, although improving, have struggled to make their mark on the international stage and are still waiting for that all-important first victory in Dhaka. The final test to take place at the Bangabandhu was the drawn game against Zimbabwe in

January 2005, leaving the home side 1–0 winners in the two-match series.

The SBNC—Shere-e-Bangla National Cricket—Stadium, named after A.K. Fazlul Haque (Shere-e-Bangla, ort the 'Tiger of Bengal'), a renowned leader in the 1940s, is outside the centre of Dhaka in Mirpur and the move there from the National Stadium was not without difficulties. The ground hosted its first test when Bangladesh played India in May 2007.

LEFT: View of the Bangabandhu Stadium during the second ODI on 10 November 2003. Since 2005 it has been used exclusively for football. *Clive Rose/Getty Images 2714921*

ABOVE: Groundsmen work on the pitch of the new Shere-e-Bangla National Stadium at Mirpur in Dhaka on 7 December 2006. Zimbabwe lost to Bangladesh on 8 December, in their fourth ODI, and the host team led the five-match series 4–0. *Farjana K. Godhuly/AFP/Getty Images 72760168s1*

BULAWAYO—QUEENS SPORTS CLUB

QUEENS SPORTS CLUB

Address: Bulawayo, Zimbabwe
Capacity: 9,000
Opening Date: 1890s

Memorable Moments:
1994 First test against Sri Lanka
1996 Zimbabwe win first ODI by two wickets
2001 Guy Whittall scored 112 in victory over Bangladesh
2004 Sri Lanka score ground's highest (731) including 438 for the second wicket (M.S. Atapattu 249, K.C. Sangakkara 270*). Sri Lanka won by an innings and 254 runs

The Queens Sports Club is home to the Matabeleland Cricket Association and first witnessed test action in October 1994. As test venues go it could be viewed as rather small but it meets local needs, possessing a charm not lost on visiting supporters.

The historic pavilion faced by the scoreboard is an excellent viewing point and, although there are uncovered stands, the popularity of the substantial grass embankments shaded by trees is easy to understand.

That first test was played against Sri Lanka and the home side opened their account with a very healthy 462 for 9 declared, captain David Houghton making 266. The opposition were forced to follow on but Zimbabwe were unable to force the win. When England visited two years later, Andy Flower top-scored

with 112 in a creditable first-innings total of 376, John Crawley and Nasser Hussain notched a century apiece in reply and a second-innings batting collapse from the tourists ensured an exciting finale.

Positive test results have almost been non-existent for Zimbabwe, but in 2001 an innings' victory over Bangladesh came as something of a tonic. Subsequently, Bulawayo has seen some pretty sorry performances, heavy losses by an innings com-

ing against West Indies in 2001 and Sri Lanka in 2004, the latter match being dominated by an innings of 270 from Kumar Sangakkara. In September 2005 the Indians inflicted another innings' defeat upon the home team, Ganguly and Laxman causing most of the damage.

HARARE SPORTS CLUB

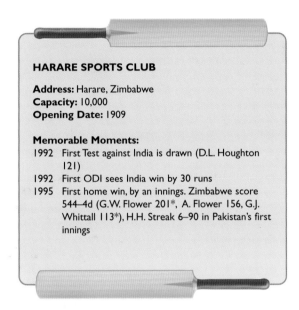

HARARE SPORTS CLUB

Address: Harare, Zimbabwe
Capacity: 10,000
Opening Date: 1909

Memorable Moments:
1992 First Test against India is drawn (D.L. Houghton 121)
1992 First ODI sees India win by 30 runs
1995 First home win, by an innings. Zimbabwe score 544–4d (G.W. Flower 201*, A. Flower 156, G.J. Whittall 113*), H.H. Streak 6–90 in Pakistan's first innings

The former Salisbury Sports Club is situated in the centre of the city, flanked by the Royal Harare Golf Club and the presidential palace.

Its capacity is rarely reached, the biggest names in the game failing to attract substantial crowds. Yet records show that in 1956 the Rhodesia/MCC game drew 26,000. The capacity can be increased by the installation of temporary stands but this is purely an academic issue in the present climate.

The gabled pavilion is a wonderful structure that would grace any ground and reportedly houses an excellent bar. At the opposite end, Castle Corner also maintains a popular bar which is a little more raucous in nature. The covered grandstand, a couple of grass embankments and a huge scoreboard complete the picture—apart, that is, from the jacaranda trees which encircle the location. Since 1992, the Harare Sports Club has been Zimbabwe's first-choice venue for Test Matches and one-day internationals. The first Test Match against India started promisingly for the home side, David Houghton scoring 121 out of a total of 456, but the weather intervened to make a winning start impossible. Less than three years later Pakistan became Zimbabwe's first victims as they slumped to an innings' defeat in the wake of some fine batting from Grant Flower and his brother Andy, who scored 201 and 156 respectively in a declared total of 544. Successes have not been plentiful in Harare in recent years, as the Zimbabweans continue to struggle when they meet the very best sides.

INDEX